W0037270

▶ **Feeling Present in the Physical World and in Computer-Mediated Environments**

DOI: 10.1057/9781137431677.0001

# Palgrave Studies in Cyberpsychology

Series Editor: **Jens Binder, Nottingham Trent University, UK**

*Titles include*

John Waterworth and Giuseppe Riva
FEELING PRESENT IN THE PHYSICAL WORLD AND IN COMPUTER-MEDIATED
ENVIRONMENTS

*Forthcoming*

Sandy Schumann
HOW THE INTERNET SHAPES COLLECTIVE ACTIONS

Christian Happ & André Melzer
EMPATHY AND VIOLENT VIDEO GAMES

Palgrave Studies in Cyberpsychology
**Series Standing Order ISBN 978–1–137–44948–1 hardback**
(*outside North America only*)

You can receive future titles in this series as they are published by placing a standing order. Please contact your bookseller or, in case of difficulty, write to us at the address below with your name and address, the title of the series and the ISBN quoted above.

Customer Services Department, Macmillan Distribution Ltd, Houndmills, Basingstoke, Hampshire RG21 6XS, England

DOI: 10.1057/9781137431677.0001

palgrave▸pivot

# Feeling Present in the Physical World and in Computer-Mediated Environments

▶

John Waterworth
*Umeå University, Sweden*

and

Giuseppe Riva
*Catholic University of Milan, Italy*

DOI: 10.1057/9781137431677.0001

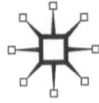

© John Waterworth and Giuseppe Riva 2014

All rights reserved. No reproduction, copy or transmission of this publication may be made without written permission.

No portion of this publication may be reproduced, copied or transmitted save with written permission or in accordance with the provisions of the Copyright, Designs and Patents Act 1988, or under the terms of any licence permitting limited copying issued by the Copyright Licensing Agency, Saffron House, 6–10 Kirby Street, London EC1N 8TS.

Any person who does any unauthorized act in relation to this publication may be liable to criminal prosecution and civil claims for damages.

The authors have asserted their rights to be identified as the authors of this work in accordance with the Copyright, Designs and Patents Act 1988.

First published 2014 by
PALGRAVE MACMILLAN

Palgrave Macmillan in the UK is an imprint of Macmillan Publishers Limited, registered in England, company number 785998, of Houndmills, Basingstoke, Hampshire RG21 6XS.

Palgrave Macmillan in the US is a division of St Martin's Press LLC, 175 Fifth Avenue, New York, NY 10010.

Palgrave Macmillan is the global academic imprint of the above companies and has companies and representatives throughout the world.

Palgrave® and Macmillan® are registered trademarks in the United States, the United Kingdom, Europe and other countries.

ISBN: 978-1-137-43168-4  EPUB
ISBN: 978-1-137-43167-7  PDF
ISBN: 978-1-137-43166-0  Hardback

A catalogue record for this book is available from the British Library.

A catalog record for this book is available from the Library of Congress.

www.palgrave.com/pivot

DOI: 10.1057/9781137431677

# Contents

DOI: 10.1057/9781137431677.0001

DOI: 10.1057/9781137431677.0001

# List of Illustrations

## Figures

## Tables

DOI: 10.1057/9781137431677.0002

# 1
# The Importance of Feeling Present

**Abstract:** *Chapter 1 opens the book with a brief discussion of the meaning of presence and why it is important. The sense of presence is characterized as a basic state of consciousness – the conscious feeling of being located in an external world, at the present time. This applies to the physical world in which our bodies are located, to virtual worlds created through technological mediation, and to blended mixture of the two – the physical and the virtual. Attention is drawn to the fact that, since technology is quickly changing and proliferating in our lives, presence is itself evolving into new forms, some of which are discussed later. The chapter closes with an outline of the overall scope and content of the book.*

Waterworth, John and Giuseppe Riva. *Feeling Present in the Physical World and in Computer-Mediated Environments*. Basingstoke: Palgrave Macmillan, 2014. DOI: 10.1057/9781137431677.0003.

# The meaning of presence

This book presents an evolutionary account of the *sense of presence* in physical and computer-mediated environments. We characterize the sense of presence as a basic state of consciousness – the conscious feeling of being in an external world, at the present time. This applies to the physical world in which our bodies are located, to virtual worlds created through technological mediation, and to blended mixture of the two – the physical and the virtual. We provide a model for understanding why we sometimes feel present in these places, why we sometimes do not, and why it matters. We start the story with a question.

Do you really feel *present* in the place your body is located right now? In other words, do you feel a sense of your own presence in your current physical surroundings? Almost certainly yes, since you were just asked the question. And at least to some extent just before that, unless you were asleep; but then again, maybe not all that much. The extent to which you feel present in the world depends on where your attention is focused and why. Is your awareness really occupied by what is happening around you, so that you are mentally present? Or are you more absorbed in your own thoughts, plans, memories – or even this book – in which case you are more or less mentally absent from your current location? In our daily life we constantly move between mental presence and absence in response to the practicalities of our situation, balancing the need to attend to the immediate environment with the need to think about what we are doing, have done, or are going to do.

Let's take an extreme example. Imagine you are sitting in a lecture hall listening to a speaker, but the speech is terribly boring. You try to listen to it, to be mentally present in the room, but your attention just wanders away and towards thinking about the fun that you had on a night out the previous evening. For a while, the lecture hall is little or no part of your experience, and you have become what we label as *absent*. Then the hardness of the seating and the coldness of the lecture hall draw your attention back to the room you are physically in, and you become some-what present. You try again to take in what the speaker is saying, but this time you drift off into thinking about what to have for dinner and the shopping you are going to have to do on the way home. And so it goes on until, suddenly, a crazed-looking person crashes into the room near the speaker, and moves towards the audience wielding a large axe, which

DOI: 10.1057/9781137431677.0003

appears to be dripping blood. In an instant, and for the first time that afternoon, you are totally present in the room.

The story above illustrates that how present you feel varies widely according to events, to your activities, interests, moods, and energy levels, amongst many other things. It varies from day to day, and even moment by moment, as in the situation just described. This is entirely normal and necessary. To function effectively requires appropriate levels of presence and absence over time, as events unfold according to changing external and personal circumstances. An imbalance in the relative levels of presence and absence is reflected in ineffective, non-adaptive, and sometimes physically hazardous behaviour. To function effectively, our focus of attention must shift appropriately between the outside world and the private world of thoughts, plans and memories, and we must be able to feel the difference. The ability to feel this is the sense of presence.

Our experiences in daily life are increasingly mediated by information technology and communication technologies, and our experience of presence is often a result of this. The task of maintaining a balance between presence and absence has changed dramatically with the widespread adoption of electronic devices such as mobile phones, tablet computers, wearable devices and large screen displays. For example, we are surrounded by people walking while texting in the street or phoning while driving their cars, and we all are doing the same. Digital devices provide us with information and experiences wherever we are, so that the task of balancing presence and absence has changed – and it will continue to change. Any consideration of the nature and future of human experience needs to take account of the importance of this *mediated presence*. Mediated presence is the feeling of being in an external world, in the realization of which information and communication technologies play a role. The immediate world in which we all live is a mediated world.

Interest in the sense of presence was initially stimulated by the widely reported sensation experienced during the use of interactive virtual reality (VR) environments, of "being there" – of (to some degree) feeling that one is actually physically present within the portrayed but virtual reality. Initially this mediated presence was called *telepresence*, because it was primarily seen as a technology-induced illusion of being present in one (simulated) place when one is actually present in another (physical) place. Mediated presence is most obviously a key element in our experience of media such as interactive games and therapeutic virtual realities. When we experience strong mediated presence, our experience is that

DOI: 10.1057/9781137431677.0003

the technology has become part of the self, and the mediated reality part of the world in which we exist.

When we feel strong mediated presence, we react emotionally and bodily (at least to some extent) as if the virtual world existed physically. But while interest in mediated presence was aroused by the development of virtual reality technology in the 1990s, it has now expanded to other forms of interactive experiences and situations, and indeed to the experience of digital media in general. As Biocca (1997) pointed out, "while the design of virtual reality technology has brought the theoretical issue of presence to the fore, few theorists argue that the experience of presence suddenly emerged with the arrival of virtual reality."

We suggest that the sense of presence is the result of an evolved neuropsychological process, created through the evolution of the central nervous system, to solve a key problem for survival: How to differentiate between the internal (the self) and the external (the other)? The strength of the feeling of presence reflects the extent to which conscious attention is focused on the non-self, the other, and variations in the strength of this feeling provide vital information for survival. This fundamental animal ability has developed in humans into the ability to distinguish external, physical events and situations from events and situations realized mentally, in thought and imagination. This is a necessary distinction that cannot be made on the basis of emotional appraisal or reality judgements, because imagined situations trigger the same emotional responses as physical situations (Russell, 1996) and may also be judged real or unreal (as may physical events).

From a survival standpoint, it is obviously vital for all sentient creatures to respond rapidly to present threats and opportunities in the environment, through the appropriate allocation of attention. Our perspective is that the sense of presence as a mental faculty was designed by evolution to ensure that organisms know when they are attending to the *external* world – to things in their here and now that might affect their survival. This is the case even though, and because, they use much of the same mental machinery to generate *internal* worlds and their experiences of them. To be able to do this, they need to *feel directly* when they are attending to the current external world – and this is the feeling of presence. Mistaking thoughts for actions or vice versa is a serious, and potentially fatal, error or mental processing. The feeling of presence is in our view analogous to feeling emotion; it is informative, direct, and has

DOI: 10.1057/9781137431677.0003

a long evolutionary history. It is closely bound up with the intention to act, of mental and bodily readiness for action in the world.

## The evolution of mediated presence

As more and more of our experiences are mediated by digital information and communication technology, it is reasonable to see the future of the human sense of presence as reflecting the rapid development of ever more pervasive digital technologies, which will increasingly mediate our experiences in the future. As we increasingly come to rely on mediated experiences, the circumstances for our feelings of presence will change. The ways in which our sense of presence develops in the future will thus reflect the evolution of consciousness through technological mediation.

Currently, we can see two main trends in the evolution of presence: VR and blended reality. Interest in the topic of presence was initially stimulated by the development of immersive and convincing virtual realities in the 1980s and 1990s, and spread more generally to immersive media such as surround sound and vision systems and stereoscopic movies. VR applications were successfully developed for various purposes, including artistic, educational and – of special interest to the themes in this book – psychotherapeutic. With falling technology prices more people installed richly sensory cinema systems at home, and many 3D movies have been released for these and for high-tech cinema viewing. Despite this, truly immersive VR responsive to head and body movements and with low-latency stereoscopic displays did not reach a mass market, largely because of the costs and complexities involved. This seems to be changing with the emergence of relatively low-cost but highly effective movement-sensitive head-mounted displays, in particular the Oculus Rift™ recently developed by Oculus VR®.

The other trend in presence is towards capitalizing on our hereditary capacity for presence in the physical world by embedding the virtual within it, in so-called *blended reality*. The emergence of ambient displays, tangible interaction objects, environmentally embedded sensors and a variety of location and state-sensitive mobile devices have made it possible for the physical and the virtual to be combined as never before, in a way that allows our natural sense of presence in the physical world to be preserved (potentially, at least) while we also deal with virtual entities, distant people, and other digitized sources of information.

DOI: 10.1057/9781137431677.0003

The smart location-aware mobile phone, with multiple functions including internet, television and other media access, is the most obvious example of information technology penetrating ever more pervasively into our everyday lives and affecting our feelings of presence. And there are many others, including those in the home, the car, and the office. When using most existing products of this type there is competition for the user's conscious attention between the physical and the digital worlds, still representing a potentially dangerous conflict. This is why, for example, using a mobile phone while driving is illegal in many countries. This is not only a conflict between presence here and presence there, but often also a conflict between self and other, presence and absence – since the right balance of the two is necessary for effective action in the world.

The future effect on consciousness of the rapid evolution of ever more pervasive digital technologies is often interpreted in terms of three inter-related arguments. The first is that the technology in general is increasingly part of our selves: not only embedded devices such as pacemakers or electrodes on the brain, but also carried devices such as mobile phones and even laptops are all parts of us – and we are (and always have been) cyborgs (e.g. Clark, 2003). The second is that "embodied" interaction characterizes our future with information technology (Dourish, 2001) through tangible interaction. In tangible interaction, physical objects are used to represent virtual entities and are manipulated bodily (usually manually) to interact with information systems, creating a kind of mixed reality space. For example, images may be projected by a computer system onto the surfaces of physical objects or manikins, while movements of these or other objects may also be tracked and interpreted as significant actions by the human user. The third argument is that the individual is in some ways an abstraction; the mind is already extended by information technology beyond the body, through extended perception and "distributed cognition" (e.g. Hutchins, 1996).

These views are very general – so general that they are not very useful scientifically, since they do not provide the specificity to answer the question: When does technology not become part of us? However, we can shed light on the answer through a consideration of the sense of mediated presence, and how this reflects a continuing need to distinguish self from other. Only some kinds of digital technology become part of the self. From the vantage point of an understanding of presence, we can predict which kinds of technology will become part of the self, and which will remain part of the other, the non-self – devices that we

DOI: 10.1057/9781137431677.0003

have and use, but which do not become part of us. To the extent that we feel present via a technology, that technology has become part of our embodiment.

## The scope of this book

In Chapter 2, we describe how the strength of the human feeling of presence is determined by two main factors: the extent to which conscious attention is tightly focused or more diffuse, and the degree of integration of different *layers of presence* derived from three levels of the functioning of the self: proto (proprioceptive) presence, core (perceptual) presence, and extended (reflective) presence. Maximum presence occurs when attention is tightly focused, and the three layers are integrated. Minimum presence, which we term *absence*, occurs when attention is tightly focused but the three layers are not integrated. Failures or maladjustments of the presence ability have predictable consequences in various forms of psychological distress that can be understood in terms of our model. It is from the experienced distinction between presence and absence that the therapeutic potential of new information technology derives.

In Chapter 3 we show how this evolutionary model of presence provides the missing link between two different but converging perspectives for understanding human action provided by recent research in neuroscience: the cognitive and the volitional. On one side, cognitive studies analyse how action is planned and controlled in response to environmental conditions. On the other side, volitional studies analyse how action is planned and controlled by subject's needs, motives and goals. In this chapter we suggest that the notion of presence can serve as the missing link between these two approaches. In particular, a consideration of presence can explain how we can distinguish between a perceived action, a planned and an executed one. We go on to argue that the evolutionary role of presence is the control of agency through the unconscious separation of "internal" and "external" and the enaction/reenaction of intentions. We conclude that our interpretation of the role of presence in action is beginning to be supported by evidence of the neural and other physical correlates of motor acts, imitation and self-monitoring. Another strength is that it provides testable predictions about how to improve the experience of presence in media: maximal presence in a mediated experience arises from an optimal combination of form and content, able to support the intentions of the user.

DOI: 10.1057/9781137431677.0003

Chapter 4 goes more deeply into exactly what happens with presence when action is implemented using a tool. First, we propose a taxonomy of mediated action distinguishing between "first-order mediated action", "second-order mediated action" and "second-order avatar-based mediated action". We then argue that these mediated actions through tools, when produced intuitively, have different and predictable effects on our experience of body and space (bodily self-consciousness).

Chapter 5 presents a framework for understanding the potentials for the design of individual presence through interaction. Taking the insights related to presence through tool use presented in Chapter 4, together with the idea that the sense of presence characterizes the experience of embodiment in the world (and in mediated worlds), we distinguish three general forms of mediated presence resulting from *expanded*, *altered* and *distributed* embodiment. Presence in expanded embodiment is typified by immersive VR: our sense of self expands outside the body and we feel ourselves to be in a place that is not the one in which our body is physically located. The design possibilities of VR are almost limitless. In altered embodiment, we experience presence in our physical location – but in new ways. New senses and abilities give us the possibility to radically alter our experience of the world in which we live. Location-aware technologies, cheap and ubiquitous sensors, and new forms of display make possible a designed integration of the physical and the virtual into an altered world. In distributed embodiment, our sense of presence is transferred into other persons, avatars, or forms – a strange experience with unpredictable effects but some promising potential for future applications.

With a focus on the applications of presence in social computer-mediated environments, Chapter 6 stresses the importance of distinguishing social from individual presence, but also highlights their similarities in some respects. In presence, the agent pre-reflexively controls his or her action, whereas in social presence the agent pre-reflexively recognizes and evaluates the actions of others. As with presence, the feeling of social presence is determined by two factors: the extent to which conscious attention is tightly focused or more diffuse, and the degree of integration of three different layers: *imitative social presence*, *interactive social presence*, and *empathic social presence* (in which the self and the other share the same intention). Maximum social presence produces the *group flow* that is the key to understanding group creativity in collaborative settings.

DOI: 10.1057/9781137431677.0003

Finally, in Chapter 7, we sum up our position on presence as outlined in this book, and make some speculations about the future of presence. Taken as a whole, the book summarizes and describes a coherent theoretical position on presence, one that the authors have developed over the past decade or so. It provides a way of understanding recent developments in the ever-increasing technology-based mediation of our lives, and to some extent predicting possible future developments and their psychological impact. It sets the ground for further experimentation, verification and exploration of this exciting and important topic.

DOI: 10.1057/9781137431677.0003

# 2
# The Layers of Presence

**Abstract:** *Chapter 2 explains how the strength of the human feeling of presence is determined by two main factors: the extent to which conscious attention is tightly focused or more diffuse, and the degree of integration of different* layers of presence *derived from three levels of the functioning of the self: proto (proprioceptive) presence, core (perceptual) presence, and extended (reflective) presence. Maximum presence occurs when attention is tightly focused, and the three layers are integrated by being focused on the same content. Minimum presence, which we term* absence, *occurs when attention is tightly focused but the three layers are not integrated. Failures or maladjustments of the sense of presence have predictable consequences in various forms of psychological distress that can be understood in terms of our model. It is from the experienced distinction between presence and absence that the therapeutic potential of new information technology derives.*

Waterworth, John and Giuseppe Riva. *Feeling Present in the Physical World and in Computer-Mediated Environments.* Basingstoke: Palgrave Macmillan, 2014. DOI: 10.1057/9781137431677.0004.

# Cognitive evolution and the sense of presence

Evolutionary psychology is a relatively new theoretical paradigm used to analyse how the evolution of the cognitive processes of our psyches continue to penetrate a wide-ranging area of our present-day behaviour (Buss, 1995). According to Bereczkei (2000), the evolutionary approach to psychological phenomena entails recognizing certain features of human behaviour that have been designed by natural selection to be useful for survival and reproduction in the environment in which humankind evolved. From this perspective, we can explain a wide variety of disparate behaviours and support a new kind of understanding of human nature. In line with this, an evolved psychological mechanism can be described (Buss, 1995) as a set of processes inside an organism that:

▸ Exists in the form it does because it (or other mechanisms that reliably produce it) solved a specific problem of individual survival or reproduction recurrently over human evolutionary history.

▸ Takes only certain classes of information or input, where input can be (a) either external or internal, or (b) actively extracted from the environment or passively received from the environment, and (c) where the input specifies to the organism the particular adaptive problem it is facing.

▸ Transforms that information into output through a procedure (e.g. a decision rule) in which output (a) regulates physiological activity, provides information to other psychological mechanisms, or produces manifest action and (b) solves a particular adaptive problem.

Many researchers have no problem in accepting that some key psychological features are the result of some evolutionary process, but the application of the same approach to presence has not been widespread – since presence is often considered only as a feature of modern media. Considering presence simply as a characteristic of a given medium misleads us into believing that the novelty of our modern environment *precludes* the idea of presence as adaptive, because humans today live in a culture unlike the Pleistocene environment in which human nature was (by general agreement) largely shaped. Yet, the human psyche evolved as a device for dealing with individual and social problems in this

DOI: 10.1057/9781137431677.0004

pre-ancient environment, and these problems often resemble those faced by humans in their everyday lives today. As Alexander (1990) states:

> I am suggesting that we are addicted to soap operas (and all other condensed and elaborate social dramas we call theater) because our ancestors literally endured similar circumstances in small groups of relatives and friends for thousands of generations, in which nothing was more important than experience and skill in manipulating the people and events involved, and such experience and skill came from observation as well as actual participation in particular events. (p. 264)

The words of Alexander also point to the importance of artefacts in the adaptation process. In fact, the adaptation strategy of our species is largely based on social learning and on the production and use of artefacts, whether material or symbolic (Massimini & Delle Fave, 2000). This strategy was supported by specific biological features, such as an upright bodily position, opposable thumbs, and the impressive growth of brain structures in both mass and complexity. As suggested by Crook (1980), humans evolved specific psychic processes concerned with awareness of the external world and awareness of their own internal state. The symbolic representations of the external world and of individuals themselves were formalized by means of descriptions and behavioural rules stored in the individual's central nervous system (intrasomatic level) and in tools, books, artistic, religious and other artefacts (extrasomatic level).

Our perspective in this book is that the ability to feel present in a virtual reality system – an artefact – does not differ from the ability to feel present in the physical world. One of the main ideas expressed in this book and our earlier publications on this topic is the connection between presence and its evolutionary role (e.g. Riva & Waterworth, 2003). We take the view that presence is an evolved psychological mechanism, created as part of the evolution of the central nervous system that allows it to embed sensorily referred properties into an internal functional space (Llinás, 2001). The emergence of the sense of presence allowed the nervous system to solve a key problem for its survival: how to differentiate between internal and external states (Waterworth & Waterworth, 2003). In relatively simple organisms, this separation involves only a correct coupling between perceptions and movements, but in humans it also requires the shift from meaning-as-comprehensibility to meaning-as-significance. Meaning-as-comprehensibility refers to the extent to which the event fits our view of the world (e.g. as controllable or non-random), whereas meaning-as-significance refers to the value or worth of the event for us (Janoff-Bulman & Frantz, 1997).

DOI: 10.1057/9781137431677.0004

In the rest of this chapter, we relate presence to the evolution of the conscious sense of self and suggest that three levels of selfhood, emerging over the course of human evolution (Damasio, 1999; Dolan, 1999), correspond directly to three distinct *layers of presence* (Riva et al., 2004). Our view of presence sees it as having the basic evolutionary function of allowing an organism to differentiate between the internal (the self) and the external (the other).

## The evolutionary levels of selfhood

Damasio distinguishes between a preconscious antecedent of self and two distinct notions of selfhood (Damasio, 1999; Dolan, 1999):

▸ *the proto self*: a coherent collection of neural patterns that map, moment by moment, the physical state of the organism;
▸ the *core self*: a transient entity which is continuously generated through encounters with objects;
▸ the *extended self*: a systematic record of the more invariant properties that the organism has discovered about itself permitting projections into the future.

This is illustrated schematically in Figure 2.1.

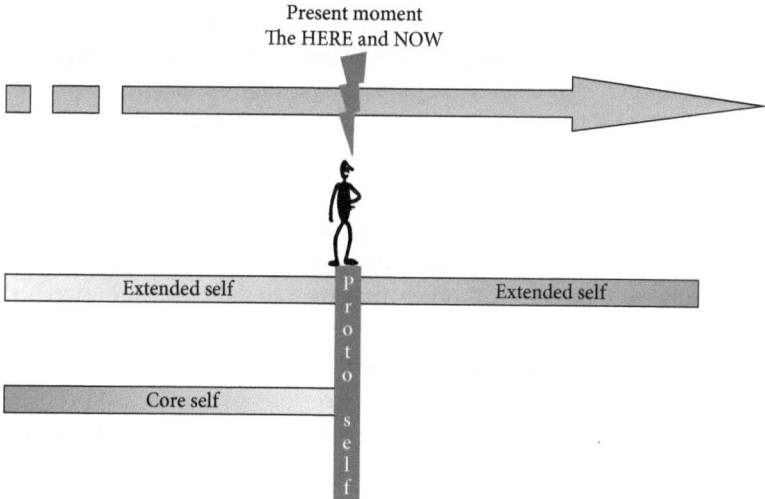

**FIGURE 2.1**   *Three components of selfhood*
Source: Riva et al. (2004).

DOI: 10.1057/9781137431677.0004

The basis for a conscious self is a feeling state that arises when organisms represent a largely non-conscious proto self in the process of being modified by objects. The core sense of self is thought to depend on the creation of a second-order mapping, in certain brain regions (brainstem nuclei, hypothalamus, medial forebrain and insular and somatosensory cortices), of how the proto self has been altered (Dolan, 1999). This gives the feeling, not just that something is happening, but that something is happening *to me*. However, it is only the autobiographical self that generates the subjective experience of possessing a trans-temporal identity (Metzinger, 1999).

When we imagine, think, plan and generally deal with information that does not only constitute our experience of things and events in the currently present external situation we are exercising extended consciousness: "Extended consciousness has to do with making the organism aware of the largest possible compass of knowledge" (Damasio, 1999, p. 198). It is extended consciousness that allows us to create an internal world in which we may suspend disbelief, as compared to a perceptual world experienced as outside the self. Extended consciousness relies on working memory, which can be seen as the "active scratchpad" of mental life (Baars, 1988; Baddeley, 2007). It is in working memory that the *internal* world we are currently experiencing is largely created. Its main function is to allow us to consider possibilities not present in the current *external* situation. In contrast, core consciousness is directed exclusively to the here and now – the present in time and space.

Extended consciousness gives us obvious advantages over organisms that lack it, such as the ability to plan and generally enact in the imagination possible scenarios of the future, as well as to increase the sophistication of learning from the past. Language depends on it, because we must retain linear sequences of symbols in working memory if we are to understand utterances, whether spoken or written, and then build an internal model of their meaning. But the advantages of extended consciousness depend on the fact that we can distinguish between the experiences of the external and the internal worlds, both remembered (things that happened) and imagined (things that didn't happen, but might). Confusions of the two indicate serious psychological problems, problems that, until recent times, would have prevented survival and the passing on of this condition.

If we react as if the external world is only imaginary we will not survive long (think of navigating a way through traffic to cross a busy

DOI: 10.1057/9781137431677.0004

street). And if we think that what we are merely imagining is actually happening, we may omit to carry out basic activities on which our survival depends (Waterworth & Waterworth, 2003). How then do we distinguish perceptions of the external world (perceptions which are themselves largely hypothetical mental predictions) from the purely mental constructions that constitute imagined situations and events? How, in other words, do we separate the internal from the external in our experiences? We suggest that presence is the feeling that evolution has given us to make this vital distinction; this is the biological purpose of presence.

## Three layers of presence

We associate a specific layer of presence with each of the three levels of self as identified by Damasio (1999). And since each layer of presence solves a particular facet of the internal/external world separation problem (which is the purpose of the sense of presence) it is characterized by specific properties. In the following parts of this section, we outline the characteristics of each layer in more detail, by focusing on its particular characteristics (see also Riva et al., 2004).

### The first layer: proto (proprioceptive) presence

As we have said, the main activity of the proto self is a largely nonconscious mapping of the physical state of the organism. The evolutionary goal of the proto self is to predict the characteristics of the external world as it is experienced through sensorial inputs.

In this process, movement plays a key role (see Figure 2.2). An adaptive movement is the evolutionary goal of the proto self, and it is only through movements that the proto self can embed properties of the external world into its proprioceptive representation. These properties are the constraints generated by the coordinate systems that describe the body. In an evolutionary process that took millions of years, the proto self was developed to experience these constraints and use them to model the external world experienced through movement.

We consider *proto presence* to be *embodied presence related to the level of proprioception-action coupling* (self vs non-self as other). The more the organism is able to correctly couple perceptions and movements, the

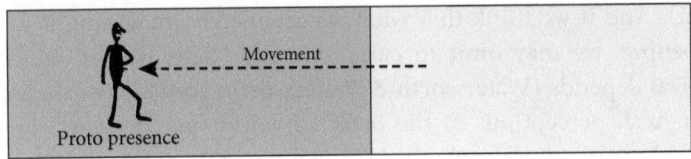

**FIGURE 2.2**    *Movement produces proto presence*
*Source*: Riva et al. (2004).

more it differentiates itself from the external world, thus increasing its probability of surviving, thus driving the evolutionary development of proto presence. An example of a situation in which proto presence would play a large role would be as follows. Imagine yourself trying to walk along a rather narrow log to cross a small river. To succeed, you must not be much concerned with the rest of the world around you, the broader surrounding environment, nor with your internal thoughts, plans and reflections. Rather your attention will be focused externally, and especially on the orientation and movement of your body in relation to the very immediate world outside.

## The second layer: core (perceptual) presence

The core self is a transient conscious entity, ceaselessly re-created for each and every object with which the organism interacts. The evolutionary goal of the core self is the integration of specific sensory occurrences into coherent percepts. This is done through a real time world model with its own internal logic (Gregory, 1997). Such perceptions depend very largely on knowledge derived from past experiences of the individual and from evolutionary history.

Distinguishing the *present* from the *imaginary* is essential for survival in the here and now. Core presence is a product of selective conscious attention to perceptions (self vs current external world as other). The more the organism is able to identify the external world and its current tasks in that world as separate from the self, the greater its probability of surviving. We suggest that core presence is needed mainly when there is a significant change in the level of core affect, so that a major shift in the level of core affect activates the possibility for a high level of core presence. Core affect is not dependent on reality judgement but responds to the contents of consciousness whether these are based on reality or imagination. This is why core presence evolved: to enable this essential distinction between the imagined and the actual. See Figure 2.3.

DOI: 10.1057/9781137431677.0004

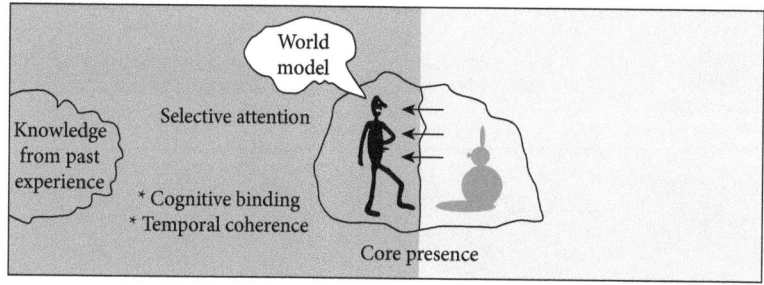

**FIGURE 2.3**   *Core presence in relation to world model and selective attention*
Source: Riva et al. (2004).

As an example of a situation where core presence would have a relatively large role, imagine that you have been walking along an undemanding footpath, passing through unexceptional, rather barren, scenery for quite some time. Suddenly, you find yourself on a large, flat, grassy promontory, providing a wide-open view of a beautiful valley, hills and a river ahead, with a wonderful sunset in progress. Your attention shifts almost exclusively to the perceptual aspects of the scene before you, and for a while you experience a relatively high degree of core presence.

## The third layer: extended (reflective) presence

The possibility of defining internal goals and tracking their achievement is the element that allows the final shift in the evolution of the self: from meaning-as-comprehensibility to meaning-as-significance. The role of extended presence is to verify the significance to the self of experienced events in the external world (self relative to the present external world as other). The more the self is present in significant experiences, the more it will be able to reach its goals, increasing the possibility of surviving (see Figure 2.4).

Imagine yourself about to take the final penalty kick in a football match, the outcome of which will determine not only the match but also a major international championship. This is the most important kick of your entire career as a footballer, one that will affect your future and that of your club for years to come. If you succeed in not being distracted by *thinking about* these aspects, the significance of the event will result in an enhanced degree of extended presence while actually taking the kick, adding extra meaning to the perceptual and bodily experiences involved in carrying out the necessary actions successfully.

DOI: 10.1057/9781137431677.0004

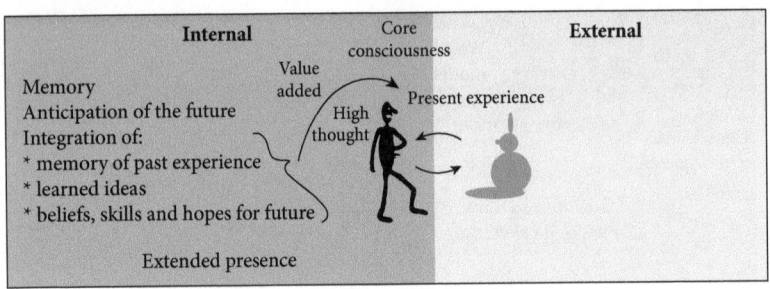

**FIGURE 2.4**    *Extended presence and meaning-as-significance*
Source:  Riva et al. (2004).

Presence is maximized when all three layers are integrated around the same external situation, whether this is physical reality, virtual reality, or a mixture of the two. When the layers are stimulated by conflicting content, however, presence will be reduced. In an awake, healthy animal in the physical world, proto presence and core presence will rarely, if ever, be in conflict. This is an aspect of presence in the physical world that is very hard to duplicate accurately with interactive media such as VR. In fact, in VR there is always some degree of conflict between these two layers and, when it is severe or the participant is particularly sensitive, so-called cyber-sickness (essentially a form of motion sickness) is a common result. In an animal possessing extended consciousness, such as humans, there will also almost always be some conflict between core presence and extended presence resulting in less than maximal presence.

## Presence and the focus of conscious attention

The sense of presence allows us to calibrate the current contents of consciousness on a continuum from total presence to total absence. Total absence is the feeling of complete absorption with the internal world of thought and imagination (the self), whereas total presence is the feeling of complete absorption in the external world (the other). Maximum presence is minimum absence from an experiential perspective, and vice versa. In people, two main factors determine how present or how absent a person feels in a specific situation: (i) the extent to which the three layers described above are integrated around the same content (as

DOI: 10.1057/9781137431677.0004

outlined in the previous section), and (ii) the extent to which conscious attention is focused on one layer or is more diffuse.

Because the three layers of presence were added progressively over the course of evolutionary development, all three layers of presence may be engaged by the external but not by the internal world (to which only extended presence applies). In other words, absence only exists for organisms possessing the capacity for extended presence, and the combinations of the two factors (above) for presence are therefore not just the converse of those for absence.

We experience maximum presence in a situation when the three layers are integrated around the same content and conscious attention is focused. This situation might occur, for example, when an expert sportsperson performs. In contrast, we experience maximum absence when conscious attention is focused but the layers are not integrated. An example of this might be when one is fully engaged in daydreaming, or in solving a difficult logical problem, while walking along an undemanding footpath. When the layers are integrated but attention is unfocused, less than maximal presence results. An example might be a novice learning a new physical skill. When attention is focused but the layers are not integrated, we experience less than maximal absence. This could be, for example, the case when we are driving a car while in a conversation.

The extent to which an individual tends to cognitively engage with the external world rather than with an internal world corresponds to aspects of individual personality. For example, we might expect that extrovert personalities in general experience – or seek to experience – higher presence than introvert personalities. Similarly, elderly people might be expected to experience less presence in common situations than the young. Although not much work has been carried out on the relationship between presence and personality, there is some evidence to support these conjectures. Laarni et al. (2004) present evidence of a positive relationship between experienced presence and extraversion, impulsivity and self-transcendence. Since Eysenck's (1967) classic characterization of the extravert as a person predominantly engaged with events in the external world, rather than the internal world of thoughts and imaginings, this is to be expected from our view of presence as a focus on the present, external environment. The same is true of impulsivity, since according to Laarni et al. (2004) impulsive individuals are better able to shift their attention in external space.

DOI: 10.1057/9781137431677.0004

We see an external attentional focus when realizing an *intention to act* in the world as the prime determinant of the feeling of presence, rather than action *per se*. Overt actions are therefore often indicators of presence, but actions can be automatized, reflex, or otherwise unconscious – or at least not bearers of intention. We need to know (to feel) when we are intending to act. Also, it has frequently been pointed out that we may experience high presence when dreaming (e.g. Biocca, 2003). In dreaming, as in waking, we experience presence according to intended actions. When dreaming while asleep much of our motor systems are immobilized to prevent damage to ourselves and those around us. In the rare cases that this defence fails, the results are shocking: we may wake up in a state of paralysis (failure to turn the defence mechanism off), or we may physically carry out deeds totally against our normal waking nature (failure to turn the defence mechanism on); see, for example, Ohayon et al. (1999). But we do not always feel very present when dreaming. Rather, we move between degrees of relative presence and absence while dreaming (as suggested by Moller and Barbera, 2006), and individuals can be expected to vary in this, as they do for waking presence. While the sense of dream presence may be experientially similar or even identical to waking presence, it differs from both physical presence and mediated presence in the low level of sensory stimulation involved in the process. Direct electromagnetic stimulation of the brain may be one way to induce something similar.

## Breakdowns in presence

The feeling of presence is not normally separated out in the experience of the subject. Rather, we experience directly significant *variations* in the level of presence. Winograd and Flores (1986) refer to *breakdowns*, which can be understood as a sudden change in presence and a disruption in action. When, during an action, an object or an environment suddenly becomes part of our consciousness rather than the action itself, a *breakdown* has occurred. Our hypothesis is that such breakdowns are an evolutionary indicator used to maintain the adaptive quality of behaviour. The sudden change in the feeling of presence tells us that something is going wrong. Errors derived from the difference between the desired state and the actual state can be used to update the model and improve performance.

DOI: 10.1057/9781137431677.0004

From a computational viewpoint, this can be explained as a *forward-inverse model* (Riva, 2009):

▶ First, the subject produces the motor command for achieving a desired state (intention – e.g. taking the apple) given the current state of the system and the current state of the environment.

▶ Second, an efference copy of the motor command is fed to a forward dynamic model that generates a prediction of the consequences of performing this motor command (action – e.g. fingers will close around the apple to lift it).

▶ Third, the predicted state is compared with the actual sensory feedback (perception – my fingers are closing around the apple). Any detected difference (e.g. the apple is too heavy and I cannot lift it) produces a breakdown.

Presence and absence are both absorption states, the former based around the current perceptual flow, the latter around imagined events and situations not currently occurring in the physical surroundings. When awake, we do not normally confuse what we conceive in imagination with what we perceive as the external world. It is our sense of presence that supports the making of this distinction; the strength of feeling of presence provides feedback on whether our attention is focused appropriately for intended actions to be successful.

Following from the above argument, many common psychological problems, such as phobias, depression, anxiety, paranoia, debilitating shyness and so on, can be seen as arising from an imbalance in the relative levels of presence and absence. We suggest that most of these problems arise as the result of too little presence, sometimes in only specific situations, sometimes more generally. The sufferers focus too exclusively on their idea of what is happening and their own place in it (their internal model of the situation or world), at the expense of experiencing their own, relatively unreflective, presence in the external situation or world.

When a person experiences a panic attack, for example, he or she initially becomes aware of the present situation (presence), but this evokes a feeling of anxiety. He or she starts to reflect on the feeling and so attention is re-directed from the external world to the internal world, for example to thinking about the self and the specific discomfort, creating a strong feeling of absence. According to dialectic behaviour therapy (Kåver & Nilsonne, 2002), one way to deal with a panic attack is for the person to direct more attention to different aspects of the external

DOI: 10.1057/9781137431677.0004

world, which will give rise to an increased and more appropriate feeling of presence.

To lose the sense of presence is to lose one's sense of being in the world, and is both an unnatural and a distressing condition. There are two obvious ways for the presence mechanism to fail: we may mistake the external for the internal or the internal for the external. The feeling that what is external is actually internal is sometimes a characteristic of depersonalization/derealization. The individual may feel that the physical world and his or her actions in it are not real. They do not feel present in the world around them. A lack of definite and appropriate presence and/or absence could relate to weak central coherence, a lack of adaptive switching between the two could relate to executive function problems, whilst a tendency towards confusion between presence and absence could relate to meta-representational failure.

Recent neuropsychological research emphasizes that most of the functioning of the motor system occurs without awareness, but that we are aware of some aspects of the current state of the system. We may prepare and try out movements in imagination, for example. These mental representations of the actual and possible states of the system are based on two sources: sensory signals from skin and muscles, and the stream of motor commands that have been issued to the system (Blakemore et al., 2002). The experience of presence is generally the outcome of a match between these two sources. I only feel myself to be present in an external world when the sensory consequences of my motor commands match their contents (Riva, 2009).

In some neurological conditions, this matching breaks down. For example, in *anarchic hand*, patients seem to be aware of the actions of their hand but do not attribute its behaviour to their intentions. The complex movements of one hand are apparently directed towards a goal and are smoothly executed, yet this is unintended (Della Sala, 2005). This condition suggests that the recognition of an intentional action can be separated from the awareness of its authorship. The patients are aware of intentional actions of the anarchic hand, which they know to be their hand, yet they disown them. According to our view, if the forward dynamic model is not able to generate a prediction of the outcome of the intention, there is a breakdown in presence and the subject will not recognize the movements as his or her own (Riva, 2008).

In another disturbance – *echopraxia* – found in some schizophrenic and autistic patients, the subject makes an impulsive and apparently automatic imitation of other people's gestures. The imitation is performed immediately, irrespective of the meaning or the nature of the gesture, and with the abruptness and speed of a reflex action. This condition suggests that the patient, recognizing an intentional action in another, mistakenly attributes it to himself or herself. According to our view, if the forward dynamic model is able to generate a prediction using the other's intention, the subjects will recognize the movements as their own (ibid.) and feel presence through their actions.

Frith and deVignemont (2005) suggest that we attribute mental states to our self or to others by adopting either an *egocentric* or an *allocentric* "stance" towards mental representations. We can relate this distinction to that between presence and absence, where presence reflects an egocentric stance, absence an allocentric one. Experienced changes in levels of presence or absence inform us of our own stance, so that we can function adaptively. Frith and deVignemont (2005) further suggest that people with Asperger's syndrome suffer from a disconnection between a strong and naive egocentric stance (presence) and a highly abstract allocentric stance (absence). Even the hallucinations and delusions that sometimes typify schizophrenia can be seen as a disturbance in error-dependent updating of inferences and beliefs about the world (Fletcher & Frith, 2009). In other words, they can be seen as the inability to experience the distinction between presence and absence.

## The healing power of presence

The sense of presence is a key feature of mental life, necessary for the survival of the organism. This view is supported by considering the seriousness of breakdowns in presence, as discussed in the preceding section. It is therefore not surprising that presence also has an important and growing role in psychotherapy.

Most therapeutic approaches attempt to enact one of two different models of change: bottom-up or top-down (Safran & Greenberg, 1991). These are clearly related to the presence/absence distinction. The top-down approach (allocentric, through absence) usually involves exploring and challenging tacit rules and beliefs that guide the processing of emotional experience. The bottom-up approach (egocentric, through presence) begins with a specific emotional experience and leads eventually to change at the verbal-representational and conceptual level. These

DOI: 10.1057/9781137431677.0004

two models of change are focused on two different cognitive systems, one for information transmission (top-down) and one for conscious experience (bottom-up), both of which may process sensory input. The existence of two different cognitive systems is clearly shown by the dissociation between verbal knowledge and task performance: people learn to control dynamic systems without being able to specify the nature of the relations within the system, and they can sometimes describe the rules by which the system operates without being able to put them into practice.

The conventional psychotherapeutic framework generally takes the top-down, allocentric route, through absence. It can be crudely described as "imagining evokes emotions and the meaning of the associated feelings can be changed through reflection and relaxation". The alternative is a bottom-up, egocentric approach through presence, where "experience evokes emotions that result in meaningful new feelings which can be reflected upon" (Kåver & Nilsonne, 2002). The conventional framework is limited by the secondary nature of the feelings evoked, based on the internal world route (the "as if body-loop"). As Damasio (1999) suggests on the basis of neurological findings, "the 'body-loop' (bottom-up) mechanism of emotion and feeling is of greater importance for the experience of real feelings than the 'as if body-loop' mechanism" (top-down) (p. 294). The alternative approach, through presence, should be more effective, because by using VR effectively it can take the external world route (Riva 2008). The "body-loop" mechanism of feeling and emotion is directly experienced in the mediated presence invoked in a convincing VR environment.

Most psychotherapies have taken the allocentric (top-down) route to emotion, simply because until the advent of customizable VR the bottom-up approach was not practical or safe. The unfortunate result is that even when exploiting new interactive technologies, psychotherapy has tended to do so within a framework that fails to capitalize on the biological priority of what evokes strong presence, using VR only to provide a fully controllable environment where reactions to a specified external situation can be evaluated (see, for example, Freeman et al., 2008).

In general, organisms must be attentive to relevant perceptions of the current external world in order to carry out successful actions in that world. Action requires information that is not available from imagination. We can see several common psychological problems, such as PTSD, depression, phobia, panic attacks, as examples of maladjustment of the normal presence mechanism. The power of presence – as we define it – in psychotherapy stems from the ability to override and reset this faulty mechanism. Technologies such as VR that evoke presence in a virtual, but still external, perceived world have great power to evoke emotional experiences that can lead to psychotherapeutically valuable changes in the individual. The important point is that they appear to be more effective than techniques that rely only on imagination. We suggest that this reflects the power of presence – seen as the feeling of being located in a perceived, external world – in developing and affecting psychological well-being.

DOI: 10.1057/9781137431677.0004

# 3
# Presence as the Link between Intention and Action

**Abstract:** *Our evolutionary model of presence provides the missing link between two different but converging perspectives for understanding human action: the cognitive and the volitional. Cognitive studies analyse how action is planned and controlled in response to environmental conditions, whereas volitional studies analyse how action is planned and controlled by subject's needs, motives and goals. Presence provides the missing link between these two approaches, and can explain how a perceived action, a planned and an executed one can be distinguished from one another. The evolutionary role of presence is presented as the control of agency through the unconscious separation of "internal" and "external" and the enactment of intentions. This view of the role of presence in action is beginning to be supported by evidence of the neural and other physical correlates of motor acts, imitation and self-monitoring. It also provides testable predictions about how to improve the experience of presence in media.*

Waterworth, John and Giuseppe Riva. *Feeling Present in the Physical World and in Computer-Mediated Environments.* Basingstoke: Palgrave Macmillan, 2014. DOI: 10.1057/9781137431677.0005.

DOI: 10.1057/9781137431677.0005

# Introduction

In this chapter we suggest that our evolutionary model of presence can provide the missing link between two different but converging perspectives for understanding human action provided by recent research in neuroscience: the cognitive and the volitional. On one side, volitional studies analyse how action is planned and controlled by subject's needs, motives and goals. On the other side, cognitive studies analyse how action is planned and controlled in response to environmental conditions. In the rest of this section, we outline some aspects and limitation of these two views, before moving on to suggest a perspective based on presence as the missing link between these two approaches.

## The volitional approach to action

The first psychological attempt to define volition comes from the work of William James. According to James (1890), we have volition when there is an idea, a representation, of what is being willed, and any conflicting ideas are absent or stopped. When this happens, the idea has the power to generate the action. Moreover, the link between the idea and the action is the result of learning: any representation of an event of which the subject has learned that it follows from a given action has the power to call for that action (ideo-motor principle). As clearly explained by James (1890), imagining an action creates a tendency to its execution, if no antagonistic mental images are simultaneously present: "Every representation of a movement awakens in some degree the actual movement which is its object; and awakens it in a maximum degree whenever it is not kept from doing so by an antagonistic representation present simultaneously in the mind" (p. 526).

In this view, goal representations are functional anticipations of action: human actions are initiated by the idea of the sensory consequences that typically result from them. There is a common criticism of this approach (Hommel et al., 2001), which is that any action is not only dependent on internal causes (goals) but on external causes as well. For instance, if we consider an action such as "obtaining a PhD in Psychology" it is obvious that this action is not only dependent on internal causes (the sensory

DOI: 10.1057/9781137431677.0005

consequences resulting from it) but on external causes as well. Furthermore, the general goal driving this action does not by itself specify the detail of the actions suited to realize them. How can I pass the General Psychology exam? How can I prepare the PhD dissertation? All of these details need to be specified by taking into account many external factors (stimuli).

One of the most interesting attempts to overcome this criticism comes from the work of the Russian psychologist Aleksey Leontjev. According to this author – usually labelled as an *Activity* theorist – the best way to understand volition is to move from the level of action to a higher level: activity (Nardi, 1996). An activity is defined as a purposeful interaction of a subject (actor) with the world. Every activity is undertaken by a subject, and is oriented towards carrying out a specific intention (object), and is always mediated by physical and social tools (artefacts). Moreover, this author (Leontjev, 1978, 1981) distinguished, within the general agency of the subject, three different levels of analysis.

▸ *Activity* is the highest level of agency: the direct answers to a specific objective of the subject. The activity of the subject moves towards the object of a specific need and terminates when it is satisfied. Specifically, an objective is a process characterizing the activity as a whole. For example, in reference to Figure 3.1, the activity is to obtain a PhD in Psychology. Any objective – for example, helping anorectic girls – is closely related to a motive – for example, the need for self-actualization – and both have to be considered in the analysis of an activity.

▸ Each activity is then translated into reality through a specific *action* or a set of *actions*. Each action is a process performed with conscious thought and effort, planned and directed towards achieving a *goal*. With reference to Figure 3.1, the activity – obtain a PhD – is translated into a set of actions: going to the library to search for the sources, preparing an index, discussing it with the tutor, and so on. Each action can be then split in sub-activities, each related to a sub-goal: searching for the books about anorexia, writing the structure of the first chapter, and so on.

▸ Actions and sub-actions are developed through *operations*: if actions are connected to conscious goals, operations are related to behaviours performed automatically. In reference to Figure 3.1, the operation of typing when preparing the index of the dissertation

DOI: 10.1057/9781137431677.0005

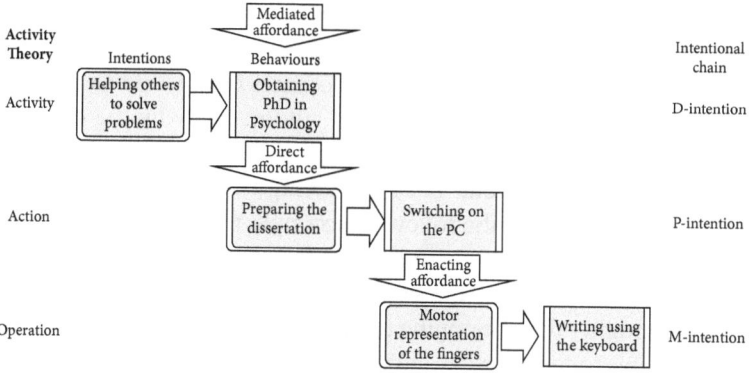

**FIGURE 3.1**    *The structure of human activity*

is done automatically, without a conscious focus on the movement of the fingers. All the operations, however, are oriented by some *conditions*: specific constrains and affordances related to the characteristics of a given tool – such as the position of the keys on the keyboard – that influence the outcome of the operation.

Conscious awareness of the conditions of a given tool is what distinguishes actions and operations. When we are learning how to use a new tool, its conditions are addressed with deliberate and conscious attention: they require actions. For instance, the first time one types, one has to consciously check the position of the letters on the keyboard. When the activity becomes well-practiced and experienced, actions do not need to be planned but are performed without conscious thought or effort: actions become operations. The opposite process is also possible: operations become actions when the original conditions are violated. For instance, if something breaks down – pressing the key does not visualize the given letter on the screen – and/or impedes execution, the subject has to consciously address (goal) the new situation using an action.

All three levels of agency are guided by anticipation, a mental representation of the final target. This anticipation is the motive of the activity, the goal of the action and the orienting basis of the operation, respectively. When the activity is performed a feedback mechanism compares the result of the activity with the prediction, and any incongruence gives rise to a learning situation.

DOI: 10.1057/9781137431677.0005

The next step of the analysis offered by *Activity Theory* is related to the link between the user and the tool. Mastering a tool has two effects for the user (Kaptelinin, 1996). First, the tool becomes transparent to the activity of the user: its conditions are handled automatically by the operations. Second, the tool is experienced as a property of the user: it complements or supports the user's abilities in improving the efficacy of the activity. Marsh (2003) provides the following example to clarify this point: "For example, a builder uses a saw to cut wood, a hammer fixes nails and joins wood, etc. In normal use, the saw and hammer become an extension of the builder rather than belonging to the external world. Consequently, the builder is able to focus on cutting the wood or driving the nail and not on the operations of (or reflect on) the saw and hammer in use" (p. 88). This specific point will be analysed in depth in Chapter 4.

## The cognitive approach to action

According to the cognitive approach to agency of American philosopher John Searle (1983), every action is made up of two components: movement and intention. The intention component "represents" the conditions that must be met by the action in order for the subject to be satisfied. Movement is the means by which the success of the intention is verified.

In Searle's words, the representation of the conditions of satisfaction refer to a "previous intention", which defines the conditions of satisfaction, and to a "background" in which they are situated (Searle, 2004). Specifically, the background includes the set of abilities, capacities, tendencies, and dispositions that humans have and use intuitively, and that are not themselves intentional states. For example, my intention to draw a house is satisfied if (a) I manage to produce a drawing and (b) what I have drawn looks like a house (in this case the background is the implicit knowledge that a house has four walls); my intention to paint my house green is satisfied if (a) I manage to paint or have the house painted and (b) the colour of the walls is green. In both cases, the background of the previous intention is the knowledge of what a house is and which house is mine.

Searle (1983) notes that there is an object, the body, which does not respect these conditions of satisfaction: my intention to move my arm is satisfied by moving my arm (auto-referential causality). In other words, if intentions regarding external objects are satisfied by the overlap between a previous intention and the result of the action, in the case of the body, the action is in itself the condition of satisfaction (*intention in action*). But

DOI: 10.1057/9781137431677.0005

how is it possible to analyse the complex network of intentions necessary to perform difficult actions such as "obtaining a degree in Psychology"? Recent cognitive studies clearly show that any action is the result of a complex intentional chain that cannot be analysed at a single level. Pacherie (2006, 2008) identifies three different "levels" or "forms" of intentions, characterized by different roles and contents: distal intentions (D-intentions), proximal intentions (P-intentions) and motor intentions (M-intentions):

▸ *D-intentions (future-directed intentions)*. These high-level intentions act both as intra- and interpersonal coordinators, and as prompters of practical reasoning about means and plans: in the activity "obtaining a PhD in Psychology" described in Figure 3.1, "helping anorectic girls" is a D-intention, the object that drives the activity of the subject.

▸ *P-intentions (present-directed intentions)*. These intentions are responsible for high-level (conscious) forms of guidance and monitoring. They have to ensure that the imagined actions become current through situational control of their unfolding: in the activity described in Figure 3.1, "preparing the dissertation" is a P-intention.

▸ *M-intentions (motor intentions)*. These intentions are responsible for low-level (unconscious) forms of guidance and monitoring: we may not be aware of them and have only partial access to their content. Further, their contents are not propositional: in the activity described in Figure 3.1, the motor representations required to move the pen are M-intentions.

Any intentional level has its own role: *the rational (D-intentions), situational (P-intention) and motor (M-intention) guidance and control of action.* They form an intentional cascade (Pacherie, 2006, 2008) in which *higher intentions generate lower intentions.*

The Centre for Cognitive Sciences in Turin, Italy, has recently become involved in the debate on the structure of intentions (Bara et al., 2011; Ciaramidaro et al., 2007; Lindner et al., 2008; Walter et al., 2005; Walter et al., 2004; Walter et al., 2009) suggesting a further distinction: the one between "private intentions" and "social intentions":

▸ *Private intentions* are all intentions that require nothing more than the intervention of the subject in order to be satisfied. Examples

DOI: 10.1057/9781137431677.0005

of this type of intentions are "removing a bulb" or "picking up an apple".

▸ *Social intentions* are all intentions which (a) involve at least one other person, and (b) the other person is essential in order for the intention to be satisfied.

  ▸ *Present social intentions* are all social intentions shared in real time by two or more subjects. The prototype of this type of social intention is communicative intentions.

  ▸ *Future social intentions* are all social intentions in which the subjects are not interacting in that moment but they will have to do so in order to satisfy their intentions. Examples of this type of social intentions are "passing a Psychology exam" or "going to buy a loaf of bread".

Ciaramidaro, Walter and their colleagues conducted a series of studies using magnetic resonance functional imaging. Thanks to these studies, carried out both on healthy subjects (Ciaramidaro et al., 2007) and subjects suffering from schizophrenia (Walter et al., 2009), it has become possible to monitor the activation of different cerebral areas according to the type of intention that the subject had to identify. Whilst private intentions only activate the precuneus and the right temporal–parietal junction, social intentions also activate the left temporal–parietal junction and the front paracingulate cortex.

In addition to the research of the Centre for Cognitive Sciences in Turin, we can consider Searle's views on "collective intentions" (1990). Unlike other social intentions, collective intentions are characterized by a "sense of the other", which moves from being an intentional subject to a collaborative subject and is then able to share the collective intention and collaborate in its realization. As well as entailing the role of another in order to be satisfied, collective intentions call for a form of cooperation that is not the result of individual intentions. These intentions (We-intentions), which can be expressed as "We intend to do action A", include one or more private or social intentions which represent a subject's personal contribution to the collective action: "I intend to do action B as part of the group's action A". An example of a collective intention is a husband and wife who intend to assemble the bed they have just bought at IKEA: it is their shared intention that directs and organizes the individual activities of the two subjects.

DOI: 10.1057/9781137431677.0005

After having carried out this analysis it is possible to propose a structure of intentions that has seven levels (see Table 3.1). These seven levels represent three different types of intentions:

▸ **Motor intentions:** motor intentions are at the basis of our most simple motor actions (not directed towards an object) such as making a fist or closing your mouth. They are innate as they are part of our genetic make-up.

▸ **Private, social and collective proximal intentions:** proximal intentions are at the basis of actions directed towards states, objects or subjects in our present world. They may be private – "pick up the pen" or "get up from the chair" – social – "climb on daddy's shoulders" or "suckle at mother's breast" – or collective – "communicate". These intentions come about in the relationships

**TABLE 3.1**   *Seven levels of intentions*

| Intention | Definition | Example |
|---|---|---|
| Motor intentions | Simple motor acts not directed towards an object | Making a fist or closing your mouth |
| Private proximal intentions | Motor acts directed towards objects or states in the present world | Picking up a pen or getting up from the chair |
| Social proximal intentions | Motor acts directed towards subjects, objects or states in the present world | Climbing on daddy's shoulders or suckling at mother's breast |
| Collective proximal intentions | Motor acts collectively directed towards subjects, objects or states in the present world | Communicating or completing a puzzle together |
| Private distal intentions | Acts directed towards objects/states in a possible world | Studying more or eating less |
| Social distal intentions | Acts directed towards objects/states in a possible world | Getting a degree or starting a family |
| Collective distal intentions | Acts organized collectively and directed towards objects/states in the present world | Winning the university football tournament or preparing a communications project together |

DOI: 10.1057/9781137431677.0005

between our needs and our surrounding physical and social environment.

▸ **Private and social distal intentions**: distal intentions are at the basis of our actions towards possible states, objects and subjects in possible worlds. These intentions may be private – such as "study more" or "do more physical exercise" – social such as "get a degree" or "start a family" – or collective – "win the university football tournament" or "prepare the communications project for the X society". These intentions come about in the relationships between our needs and the various possibilities open to us in our culture of reference.

## The role of presence in action

If we compare our short description of the volitional and cognitive approaches, we can find some interesting similarities. Both analyse agency through a three-level chain of objects/intentions in which higher levels generate lower ones. Both evaluate an action as successful through the comparison of the objects/intentions driving the action with its outcome. And both consider the mastering of a tool as the way to make it transparent (directly present) to the subject. Nevertheless, neither of them identifies a specific cognitive process addressing the complex task of comparing in real time and unconsciously the objects/intentions driving the action with its outcomes.

The first noteworthy element that emerges from the analysis of the proposed intentional structure is that understanding another's actions becomes increasingly difficult as we move from motor to distal to private and social intentions.

The second element which comes to light is that the greater complexity required by intentions of a higher level is not only reflected in the comprehension of the other's intentions but also in the judgement of the efficacy of one's own actions. More exactly, how can a subject verify whether his or her intentions have really been transformed into an effective action?

To determine whether or not one's actions have been effective is a crucial element for the survival of the individual. Without the ability to verify whether one's actions have been correctly performed – Have I managed to get the food that I need? Have I escaped from the predator

DOI: 10.1057/9781137431677.0005

who was chasing me? – the subject would not be able to survive the dangers of his or her environment. To overcome this limitation we specify the concept of presence in a particular way. As indicated earlier, we consider presence as a neuropsychological phenomenon, evolved from the interplay of our biological and cultural inheritance, whose goal is the enaction of volition. But what is its foundation in terms of the cognitive processes involved in it? In the next section we suggest that presence is an intuitive metacognitive judgement that monitors our actions: presence is *the prereflexive (intuitive) perception of successfully transforming intentions into action (enaction)*. For each intentional level – motor, proximal and distal – exists a specific layer of presence monitoring it.

## Presence is an intuitive process

Recent research in cognitive psychology underlines the role of non-conscious mental structures and processes in driving the subject's experience, and action. For example, Daniel Kahneman (2002), a psychologist who in 2002 was awarded the Nobel Prize in Economics for his work on the psychology of intuitive beliefs and choices, identified two generic modes of cognitive function: "In the terminology that became accepted much later, we held a two-system view, which distinguished intuition from reasoning... an intuitive mode in which judgments and decisions are made automatically and rapidly, and a controlled mode, which is deliberate and slower" (pp. 449–450).

Stanovich and West (2000) noted that in the past forty years, different authors from different disciplines suggested a two-process theory of reasoning based on intuitive and rational processes. Even if the details and specific features of these theories do not always match perfectly, nevertheless they share the following properties:

▸ Intuitive operations are faster, automatic, effortless, associative, and difficult to control or modify.
▸ Rational operations, instead, are slower, serial, effortful, and consciously controlled.

One of the theories based on this distinction is the cognitive-experiential self-theory (CEST). As explained by Epstein (2008):

A fundamental assumption in CEST is that people operate by two cognitive systems: an "experiential system", which is a nonverbal automatic learning

DOI: 10.1057/9781137431677.0005

TABLE 3.2    *Differences between the intuitive and rational systems according to the cognitive-experiential self-theory*

|  | Experiential/intuitive system | Rational system |
|---|---|---|
| Main features | **Intuitive**: preconscious, automatic, and intimately associated with affect<br>**Concrete**: encodes reality in images, metaphors, and narratives<br>**Associative**: connections by similarity and contiguity<br>**Rapid processing**: oriented towards immediate action<br>**Resistant to change**: changes with repetitive or intense experience<br>**Differentiated**: broad generalization gradient; categorical thinking<br>**Integrated**: situationally specific; organized in part by cognitive–affective modules<br>**Experienced passively and preconsciously**: we are seized by our emotions<br>**Self-evidently valid**: "experiencing is believing" | **Rational**: conscious, deliberative and affect free<br>**Abstract**: encodes reality in symbols, words, and numbers<br>**Analytic**: connections by cause-and-effect relations<br>**Slower processing**: capable of long delayed action<br>**Less resistant to change**: can change with speed of thought<br>**More highly differentiated**: nuanced thinking<br>**More highly integrated**: organized in part by cross-situational principles<br>**Experienced actively and consciously**: we believe we are in control of our thoughts<br>**Not self-evident**: requires justification via logic and evidence |
| How it works | *Operates by* **hedonic principle** (what feels good)<br>Acquires its schemas by **learning from experience**<br>**Outcome oriented**<br>**Behaviour mediated by "vibes"** from past experience | *Operates by* **reality principle** (what is logical and supported by evidence)<br>Acquires its beliefs by **conscious learning and logical inference**<br>More **process oriented**<br>**Behaviour mediated by conscious appraisal** of events |

system, and a "rational system," which is a verbal reasoning system. The experiential system operates in a manner that is preconscious, automatic, nonverbal, imagistic, associative … and its schemas are primarily generalizations from emotionally significant intense or repetitive experience … In contrast to the automatic learning of the experiential system, the rational system is a reasoning system that operates in a manner that is conscious, verbal, abstract, analytical, affect free, effortful, and highly demanding of cognitive resources. It acquires its beliefs by conscious learning from books, lectures and other explicit sources of information, and from logical inference; and it has a very brief evolutionary history. (pp. 24–25)

In sum, intuitive operations are faster, automatic, effortless, associative, and difficult to control or modify. Rational operations, instead, are

DOI: 10.1057/9781137431677.0005

slower, serial, effortful, and consciously controlled. As underlined by Koriat (2007) this distinction "... implies a separation between two components or states of consciousness – on the one hand, sheer subjective feelings and intuitions that have a perceptual-like quality and, on the other hand, reasoned cognitions that are grounded in a network of beliefs and explicit memories. It is a distinction between what one feels and senses and what one knows or thinks" (p. 301).

Contrary to common thought, however, intuition is not only innate. Research on perceptual-cognitive and motor skills shows that they are automatized through experience and thus rendered intuitive (Kihlstrom, 1987). In the case of motor skill learning, the process is initially rational and controlled by consciousness, as shown, for example, by the novice driver's rehearsal of the steps involved in parking a car: check the mirrors and blind spots; signal to the side of the space; position the car beside the vehicle I'm parking behind and so on. However, later the skill becomes intuitive and consciously inaccessible by virtue of practice, as shown, for example, by the difficulty of expert drivers to describe how to perform a complex manoeuvre to others, and by the fact that conscious attention to it actually interferes with their driving performance.

Perceptual-motor skills that are not innate – for example, driving a car – may become automatic through practice, and their operations thereby rendered intuitive. Using a metaphor derived from computer science, this process can be described as *knowledge compilation* (Kihlstrom, 1987; Selman & Kautz, 1996): a knowledge given in a general representation format (linguistic-semantic) is translated into a different one, more usable and less computationally demanding (perceptual-motor).

Are presence and telepresence intuitive or rational cognitive processes? It is evident that presence is the *outcome* of an intuitive cognitive process and that no rational effort is required to experience a feeling of presence. However, presence is different from an acquired motor skill or a behavioural disposition.

A possible path to find a better answer comes from the concept of metacognition. Koriat (2007) defines "metacognition" as "the processes by which people self-reflect on their own cognitive and memory processes (monitoring) and how they put their metaknowledge to use in regulating their information processing and behavior (control)" (p. 289). Following the distinction between intuition and reasoning, researchers in this area distinguish between *information-based* (or theory-based) and *experience-based* metacognitive judgements (Koriat, 2007; Koriat

DOI: 10.1057/9781137431677.0005

& Levy-Sadot, 1999). Information-based metacognitive judgements are based on a deliberate use of one's beliefs and theories to reach an evaluation about one's competence and cognitions: they are deliberate and largely conscious, and draw on the contents of declarative information in long-term memory.

By contrast, experience-based metacognitive judgements are subjective feelings that are product of an inferential intuitive process: they operate unconsciously and give rise to a "sheer subjective experience". An example of these metacognitive judgement is (Price & Norman, 2008): the *feeling of knowing* (knowing that we are able to recognize the correct answer to a question that we cannot currently recall), or the *feeling of familiarity* (knowing that we have encountered a given situation before, even if we don't have an explicit memory of it).

As Koriat and Levy-Sadot (1999) argued, "The cues [for these metacognitive judgements] lie in structural aspects of the information processing system. This system, so to speak, engages in a self-reflective inspection of its own operation and uses the ensuing information as a basis for metacognitive judgments" (p. 496).

In other words, we can try to describe presence as the sheer subjective experience of being in a given environment (the feeling of "being there") that is the product of an intuitive experience-based metacognitive judgement.

## Presence, intuition and simulation

What, then, is intuitively judged by presence? Research by Haggard and Clark (Haggard & Clark, 2003; Haggard et al., 2002), on voluntary and involuntary movements, provides direct support for the existence of a specific cognitive process binding intentions with actions. In their words (Haggard et al., 2002): "Taken as a whole, these results suggest that the brain contains a specific cognitive module that binds intentional actions to their effects to construct a coherent conscious experience of our own agency." (p. 385).

Other authors have also suggested a role of presence in the monitoring of action. For example, Zahoric and Jenison (1998) underlined that "presence is tantamount to successfully supported action in the environment" (p. 87); Riva and colleagues (2011) suggested that "... the evolutionary role of presence is the control of agency" (p. 24); finally, Slater and colleagues (2009) argued that "humans have a propensity to

DOI: 10.1057/9781137431677.0005

find correlations between their activity and internal state and their sense perceptions of what is going on out there" (p. 208). But how does this work, and how is this process related to intuition?

Reber (1989) suggests that: "To have an intuitive sense of what is right and proper, to have a vague feeling of the goal of an extended process of thought, to "get the point" without really being able to verbalize what it is that one has gotten, is to have gone through an implicit learning experience and have built up the requisite representative knowledge base to allow for such judgement" (p. 233). In simpler words, through implicit learning the subject is able to represent complex actions using perceptual-motor data and enact/monitor them intuitively. Important support for this view comes from the recent discovery of "bimodal" neurons.

A group of neurophysiologists from Parma, Italy, coordinated by Giacomo Rizzolatti, discovered, first in the pre-motor cortex of apes, and then in that of humans, the existence of two groups of "bimodal" neurons in which sensory faculties are linked to motor faculties (Rizzolatti & Sinigaglia, 2006):

▸ the first group of neurons (F5ab-AIP), known as *canonical* neurons, are activated when a subject sees an object with which it can potentially interact;
▸ the second group of neurons (F5c-PF), known as *mirror* neurons, are activated when the subject sees another individual performing the same action.

To justify the existence of these neurons the Common Coding Theory has been developed: according to this theory perceptual representations (actions perceived) and motor representations (actions to be performed) are based on the same motor code (Knoblich & Flach, 2003; Prinz, 1997). In practice, in each phase of a single action – *planning* (I want to move my hand to pick up an apple), *execution* (I move my hand and pick up the apple) and *interpretation* (I see another person move their hand to pick up the apple) – the subject is activating the same motor code applied to the context in which the action is being, or will be, performed.

This theory leads us to presume the existence of a simulation system based on motor codes which permits the subject to organize and under-stand a given action (Barsalou, 2003; Gallese, 2005; Wilson & Knoblich, 2005). As Gallese points out (Gallese, 2003a,b, 2005), during the simu-lation process, which he defines as "embodied simulation", internal

DOI: 10.1057/9781137431677.0005

representations of corporal objects associated with given actions and sensations are generated within the subject, as if he or she were performing a similar action or experiencing similar emotions or sensations. For example, the sight of a red apple is believed to activate a simulation of the motor functions necessary to pick it up, while the sight of a person who reaches out to pick up the apple is believed to activate a motor simulation which allows the subject to understand this person's intention.

According to *Covert Imitation Theory* (Knoblich et al., 2005; Wilson & Knoblich, 2005), the brain instantiates a sophisticated simulation, based on motor codes, of the outcome of an action and uses this to evaluate its course. This can be achieved through a simulative forward model (Blackmore & Decety, 2001; Riva, 2009): during the enaction of a learned skill a sensory prediction of the outcome of the action (simulation) is produced along with the actual motor command. The results of the comparison (which occurs intuitively) between the sensory prediction and the sensory consequences of the act can then be utilized to determine both the agent of the action and to track any possible variation in its course (see Figure 3.2). If no variations are perceived, the subject is able to concentrate on the action and not on its monitoring.

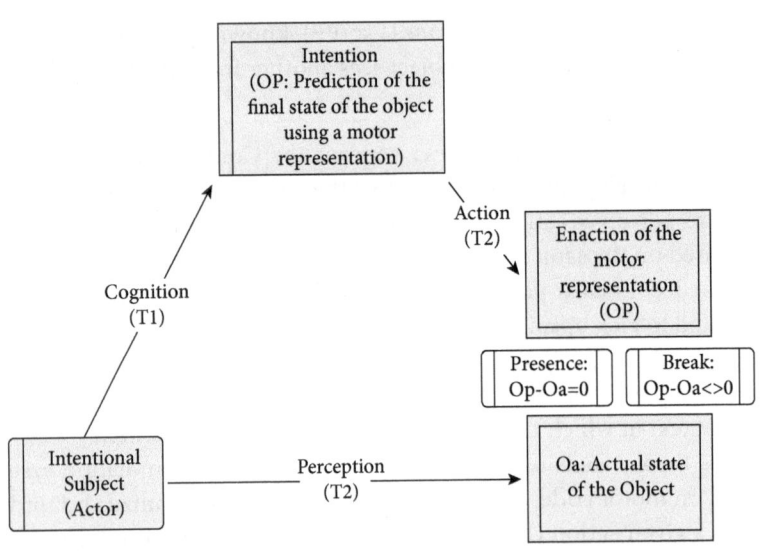

**FIGURE 3.2**  *The feeling of presence*
*Source*: adapted from Riva (2009).

DOI: 10.1057/9781137431677.0005

By this view, presence is unconscious in the sense that we do not have detailed conscious access to its processing antecedents. It is conscious, too, in that it is a distinct phenomenology — something it feels like to have the feeling. And it is metacognitive since it conveys information about our spatial experience that permits to monitor and eventually regulate our action. In summary, presence is an intuitive experience-based metacognitive judgement:

▶ It monitors pre-reflexively our activity processes.
▶ It is achieved using an embodied intuitive simulation of the intended action.
▶ Only when the subject acquires a motor skill he/she is able to simulate its outcome intuitively (implicit learning).
▶ A break in presence is a violation of our intuitive simulation. As a consequence the subject is forced to shift to reasoning to understand and cope with the causes of the violation.

A possible criticism to this vision is the following (Riva, 2009): "What about this thought experiment: paint a 20' by 20' by 20' room completely white, there are no windows, have a person sit in the middle of the room, there is nothing to interact with, is the person not present there?" (p. 61). The answer to this criticism is to be found in the word "intuitive". Even to stand, sit, or to lie down on a floor, the involvement of different intuitive postural processes that we learned in our first months of life is required. For example, a newly born infant learns to sit independently only between the ages of four and seven months. When these intuitive postural processes do not work as it happens, for example, experiencing an *isolation tank* – a lightless, soundproof tank in which subjects float in salty water at skin temperature (see an example on YouTube at http://www.youtube.com/watch?v=YEjTXX2rHgA) – within 15/20 minutes the feeling of presence totally disappears (Kjellgren et al., 2004).

A second possible criticism is the following: "Intuitive thinking is error prone yet my experience of being in the world is not. How can we account for this?"

A first answer to this question is related to the simulative forward model described in Figure 3.1. According to it our brain represents sensory information probabilistically (Knill & Pouget, 2004; Vilares & Kording, 2011) in the form of probability distributions. As empha-sized by Knill and Pouget (2004): "This allows the system to integrate information efficiently over space and time, to integrate information

DOI: 10.1057/9781137431677.0005

from different sensory cues and sensory modalities, and to propagate information from one stage of processing to another without committing too early to particular interpretations ... [In sum], humans behave near-optimally even when the sensory information is characterized by highly non-Gaussian density functions, leading to complex patterns of predicted behavior" (pp. 712 and 718).

An answer to this second criticism is that our experience of the world is error prone, even if we are not aware of it. In their book *The Invisible Gorilla: How Our Intuitions Deceive Us* Chabris and Simons (2010) describe how our experience is full of "gaps" or "illusions" in six different areas: attention, memory, confidence, knowledge, cause and potential. The most significant example for the goals of this chapter is the one described in the title of the book: *The Invisible Gorilla*. In an experiment the two authors asked their sample to watch a one-minute video of a basketball game and to count the number of passes made by the team wearing white. During the video a woman wearing a gorilla costume walked into the scene, stopped, faced the camera and walked off. Half the sample did not see the gorilla: the gorilla was not present to them. Moreover, when asked later on, "Did you notice a gorilla?" they were unable to believe that they had missed it, and they were astonished when they watched the video again and saw it.

## Presence monitors our action and experience

We can now describe presence as a sophisticated but unconscious form of monitoring of action and experience, transparent to the self but critical for its existence. The main experiential outcome of this process is the sense of agency: we feel that we are both the author and the owner of our own actions. For this reason, the feeling of presence is not separated by the experience of the subject but it is related to the quality of agency. A higher level of presence is experienced as a better quality of action and experience: the more the subject is able to enact his/her intentions in a successful action, the more he/she feels present. As suggested by Bickard (2004): "There is much to be addressed about such systems of action selection, but the crucial point for now is that any triggering of an interaction, or any indication of the current appropriateness of an interaction, presupposes that that interaction is in fact appropriate for the current conditions" (p. 78).

We suggest that it is the *feeling of presence that provides key feedback to the self about the status of its activity*. The self perceives the variations in

DOI: 10.1057/9781137431677.0005

the feeling of presence and tunes its activity accordingly. This tuning is achieved through a simulative forward model (Blakemore & Decety, 2001): during self-produced actions a sensory prediction of the outcome of the action is produced along with the actual motor command. The results of the comparison (which occurs at a sub-personal level) between the sensory prediction and the sensory consequences of the act can then be utilized both to determine the agent of the action and to track any possible variation in its course. If no variations are perceived, the self is able to concentrate on the action and not on its monitoring. As suggested by *Covert Imitation Theory* (Knoblich et al., 2005; Wilson & Knoblich, 2005), the brain instantiates a sophisticated simulation, based on motor codes, of the outcome of an action and uses this to evaluate its course.

For this reason, the feeling of presence – *the prereflexive perception that the agent's intentions are successfully enacted* – is not separated by the experience of the subject but *is directly related to it*. It corresponds to what Heidegger (1959) defined as "the interrupted moment of our habitual standard, comfortable *being-in-the-world*". A higher feeling of presence is experienced by the self as a better quality of action and experience (Zahoric & Jenison, 1998). The agent perceives directly only *significant variations* in the feeling of presence: *breakdowns* and *optimal experiences* (Riva, 2006). These are taken up in more detail in the next chapter (Chapter 4).

Why do we consciously track presence variations? Our hypothesis is that this is a sophisticated evolutionary tool used to control the quality of behaviour. Specifically, the subject tries to overcome any breakdown in its activity and searches for engaging and rewarding activities (optimal experiences). It provides both the motivation and the guiding principle for successful action. According to Csikszentmihalyi (1975, 1990), individuals preferentially engage in opportunities for action associated with a positive, complex and rewarding state of consciousness, defined by him as "optimal experience" or "flow". There are exceptional situations in which the subject experiences a higher level of presence than in most others. In these situations the subject experiences a full sense of control and experiential immersion. When this experience is associated with a positive emotional state, it constitutes a flow state. An example of flow is the case where a professional athlete is playing exceptionally well (positive emotion) and achieves a state of mind where nothing else is attended to but the game (high level of presence).

DOI: 10.1057/9781137431677.0005

It follows from the views presented in this chapter that it is possible to design mediated situations that elicit a state of flow by activating a high level of presence (maximal presence) (Gaggioli et al., 2013; Morganti & Riva, 2004; Riva, 2004; Waterworth et al., 2003). The relationship between presence and the use of tools to enact intentions is discussed in more detail in the next chapter, Chapter 4. We explore the wider possibilities and implications of designing for individual presence in Chapter 5.

DOI: 10.1057/9781137431677.0005

# 4

## Presence, Digital Tools and the Body

**Abstract:** *What happens to presence when action is implemented using a digital tool? A taxonomy of mediated action is presented, distinguishing between first-order mediated action, second-order mediated action and second-order avatar-based mediated action. When produced intuitively these mediated actions have different effects on our experience of body and space (bodily self-consciousness). A successfully learned first-order mediated action produces* incorporation, *in which the proximal tool extends the peripersonal space of the subject. A successfully learned second-order mediated action produces* incarnation, *a second peripersonal space centred on the distal tool. When a successfully learned second-order mediated action is implemented through an avatar this may, under certain conditions, produce* embodiment *as the tool, in which the user actually feels present as the avatar.*

Waterworth, John and Giuseppe Riva. *Feeling Present in the Physical World and in Computer-Mediated Environments.* Basingstoke: Palgrave Macmillan, 2014. DOI: 10.1057/9781137431677.0006.

# Introduction

We have described presence as a sophisticated form of monitoring of action and experience. In Chapter 3 we discussed the link between intention, action and presence. In this chapter we will analyse and discuss more deeply what happens to presence from the perspective of action implemented using a tool.

We argue here that experiencing presence in a mediated action has three possible effects on our experience of body and space (bodily self-consciousness) related specifically to the characteristics of the used tool:

▸ **Incorporation of the tool:** the tool extends the peripersonal space of the subject.
▸ **Incarnation through the tool:** the user experiences a second peripersonal space centred on the tool.
▸ **Embodiment as the tool:** the user experiences a new body in the tool.

# Bodily self-consciousness

The increasing interest of cognitive science, social and clinical psychology in the study of the experience of the body is providing an account of what our bodily self-consciousness is. As described by Olaf Blanke (2012): *"Human adults experience a 'real me' that 'resides' in 'my' body and is the subject (or 'I') of experience and thought. This aspect of self-consciousness, namely the feeling that conscious experiences are bound to the self and are experiences of a unitary entity ('I'), is often considered to be one of the most astonishing features of the human mind"* (p. 556).

Recent research work in this area is also providing some insight about the processes involved in it (Blanke, 2012; Gallagher, 2005; Slaughter & Brownell, 2012; Tsakiris et al., 2010). First, even though bodily self-consciousness is normally experienced by the subject as a unitary experience, neuroimaging and neurological data suggest that it includes different experiential layers that are integrated in a coherent experience (Blanke, 2012; Crossley, 2001; Pfeiffer et al., 2013; Shilling, 2012; Vogeley & Fink, 2003). In general, we become aware of our body through exteroceptive signals arising on (i.e. touch), or outside the body (i.e. vision) and through interoceptive (i.e. heart rate) and proprioceptive (i.e. skeletal

DOI: 10.1057/9781137431677.0006

striated muscles and joints) signals arising from within the body (Durlik et al., 2014; Garfinkel & Critchley, 2013).

Second, these studies support the idea that bodily representations play a central role in structuring cognition and the self. For this reason, the experience of the body is strictly connected to processes such as cognitive development and autobiographical memory. But what is the role of bodily self-consciousness?

We use the "feelings" from the body to sense both our physical condition and emotional state. These feelings range from proprioceptive and exteroceptive bodily changes that may be visible also to an external observer (i.e. posture, touch, facial expressions) to proprioceptive and interoceptive changes that may be not visible to an external observer (i.e. endocrine release, heart rate, muscle contractions) (Bechara & Damasio, 2005).

As suggested by Craig (2002, 2003), all feelings from the body are represented in a hierarchical homeostatic system that maintains the integrity of the body. More, a re-mapping of this representation can be used to judge and predict the effects of emotionally relevant stimuli on the body with the aim of making rational decisions that affect survival and quality of life (Craig, 2010; Damasio, 1994). According to Damasio (1994), this "collective representation of the body constitutes the basis for a 'concept' of self" (p. 239) that exists as "momentary activations of topographically organized representations"(p. 240). This view is shared by several authors. For example, for Craig (2003) "the subjective image of the 'material me' is formed on the basis of the sense of the homeostatic condition of each individual' s body" (p. 503).

## The common code of bodily self-consciousness: spatial images

A key feature of the bodily self-consciousness is its ability of processing, integrating and generating a wide range of different inputs and patterns: sensory experiences, thoughts, feelings, attitudes, beliefs, memories and imagination. For a long time brain sciences considered action, perception, and interpretation as separate activities. However, as discussed in the previous chapter, brain sciences are starting to describe cognitive processes as *embodied* (Prinz, 2006). In this view, perception, execution, and imagination share a common spatial coding in the brain (Hommel et al., 2001). When an effect is intended, the movement that produces

DOI: 10.1057/9781137431677.0006

it is automatically activated as a perceptual input, because actions and their effects are stored in a common representational domain.

*Common Coding Theory* extends this approach to the domain of event perception, action perception, and imitation. The underlying process is the following (Knoblich & Flach, 2003): first, common event representations become activated by the perceptual input; then, there is an automatic activation of the spatial codes attached to these event representations; finally, the activation of the spatial codes results in a prediction of the action results in terms of expected perceptual events on the common coding level.

Giudice and colleagues (2013) recently demonstrated that the processing of spatial representations in working memory is not influenced by its source. It is even possible to combine long-term memory data with perceptual images within an active spatial representation without influencing judgements of spatial relations.

A recent hypothesis is that these different representations can be integrated into an amodal spatial representational format, defined "spatial image" (see Figure 4.1), shared by perceptual, memory and linguistic knowledge (Baddeley, 2012; Bryant, 1997; Kelly & Avraamides, 2011; Loomis et al., 2007; Wolbers et al., 2011). Both Bryant and Loomis identified this representational format in a three-dimensional egocentric coordinate system (Bryant, 1997; Loomis et al., 2007; Loomis et al., 2013;

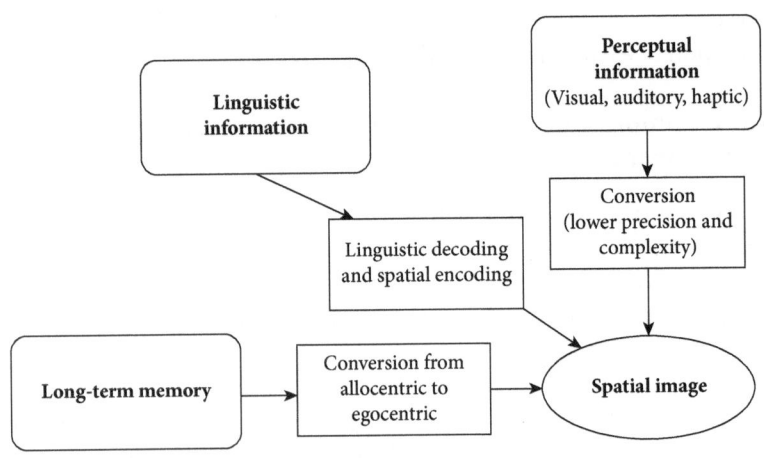

FIGURE 4.1   *Multimodal contents of spatial images*
Source: adapted from Loomis et al. 2013.

DOI: 10.1057/9781137431677.0006

Loomis et al., 2002), available in the working memory, able to receive its contents both from multiple sensory input modalities (vision, tactile, etc.) and from multiple long-term memory contents (vision, language, etc.). This view fits well with the *Convergence Zone Theory* proposed by Damasio (1989), which has two main claims. First, when a physical entity is experienced, it activates feature detectors in the relevant sensory-motor areas. During visual processing of an apple, for example, neurons fire for edges and planar surfaces, whereas others fire for colour, configural properties, and movement. Similar patterns of activation in feature maps on other modalities represent how the entity might sound and feel, and the actions performed on it. Second, when a pattern becomes active in a feature system, clusters of conjunctive neurons (*convergence zones*) in association areas capture the pattern for later cognitive use.

Damasio assumes the existence of different convergence zones at multiple hierarchical levels, ranging from posterior to anterior in the brain. At a lower level, convergence zones near the visual system capture patterns there, whereas convergence zones near the auditory system capture patterns there. Further, downstream, higher-level association areas in more anterior areas such as the temporal and frontal lobes conjoin patterns of activation *across* modalities.

In fact, a critical feature of convergence zones underlined by Simmons and Barsalou is *modality-specific re-enactments* (Barsalou, 2003; Simmons & Barsalou, 2003): once a convergence zone captures a feature pattern, the zone can later activate the pattern in the absence of bottom-up stimulation. In particular, the conjunctive neurons play the important role of reactivating patterns (*re-enactment*) in feature maps during imagery, conceptual processing, and other cognitive tasks. For instance, when retrieving the memory of an apple, conjunctive neurons partially reactivate the visual state active during its earlier perception. Similarly, when retrieving an action performed on the apple, conjunctive neurons partially reactivate the motor state that produced it.

According to this view, a fully functional conceptual system can be built on re-enactment mechanisms: first, modality-specific sensorimotor areas become activated by the perceptual input (an apple) producing patterns of activation in feature maps; then, clusters of conjunctive neurons (convergence zones) identify and capture the patterns (the apple is red, has a catching size, etc.); later the convergence zone fire to partially reactivate the earlier sensory representation (I want to take a different apple); finally this representation reactivate a pattern of

DOI: 10.1057/9781137431677.0006

activation in feature maps similar, but not identical, to the original one (re-enactment) allowing the subject to predict the action results. The result of this interpretation is the idea of a spatial–temporal framework of virtual objects directly present to the subject: *an inner world simulation in the brain*. As described by Barsalou (2002):

> In representing a concept, it is as people were being there with one of its instances. Rather than representing a concept in detached isolated manner, people construct a multimodal simulation of themselves interacting with an instance of the concept. To represent the concept they prepare for situated action with one of its instances. (p. 9)

By this view our body, too, can be considered the result of a multimodal simulation, as Margaret Wilson underlined (2006):

> The human perceptual system incorporates an emulator … that is isomorphic to the human body. While it is possible that such an emulator is hard-wired into the perceptual system or learned in purely perceptual terms, an equally plausible hypothesis is that the emulator draws on body-schematic knowledge derived from the observer's representation of his own body. (p. 221)

## The neuropsychology of subjective space

In the previous chapter we described presence as described as a sophisticated form of monitoring of action and experience. But how is the monitoring of action and experience able to produce the feeling of being in an environment? One answer follows from what we have seen in the previous section. Research data show a clear link between spatial perception, our bodily experience and action.

We conceive places in terms of the actions we could take towards them: subjects do not have separate knowledge of the place's location relative to them, what they can do in it, and their purposes. An example can help in understanding this point. Retrieving an occluded object – for example, when we lift a box to retrieve a pencil from under it – is an action taken on the basis of a belief about where the object (pencil) is located relative to the self. As noted by Waskan (2006), "one cannot see a place as being there1 rather than there2 *without knowing what it would be to act* there1 rather than there2" (p. 170, our italics). It follows that to know that the pencil exists when it is occluded is a matter of knowing what can be done to make the pencil visible. If I want to grab the pencil, its spatial position will be represented in terms of the movements needed

DOI: 10.1057/9781137431677.0006

to reach for it. Further, its shape and size will be represented in terms of the type of handgrip it affords.

Our spatial experience is the outcome of the interaction of different spatial representations whose integrated activity gives rise to spatial awareness (Matelli & Luppino, 2001). For example, the proprioceptive knowledge of our own body's location in external space (*the feeling of being in a given space*) requires that information about the angles of each joint be combined with information about the size and shape of the body segments between joints. However, as noted by Longo and Haggard (2010) the metric properties of different body parts are not directly provided by sensory signals. In other words, the experience of presence in the external space requires that the on-line proprioceptive information (i.e. body posture) are integrated by stored data related to a body model (*intrinsic body representation*) constructed by the brain. This model which is coarse-grained and relatively inaccurate – as shown by both the "phantom limb" experience and the "rubber hand" illusion – is the pillar that defines our whole spatial experience.

Evidence from clinical and experimental studies indicates that our spatial experience involves the integration of different sensory inputs within two different reference frames defined by our body model and related to its possibility of action (Galati et al., 2000; Longo et al., 2010; Previc, 1998):

▸ *Subjective/near space* (body as reference of first-person experience). It is shaped around the *egocentric frame* and its primary source is *somatoperceptions*: representations of the present state of the body and tactile stimuli from sensory inputs (Longo et al., 2010). In fact, it is based on the body of the observer: it is defined by its three axes: front-back, left-right, head-feet and within this frame the position of an object changes if the subject moves (Frith & de Vignemont, 2005). Furthermore, this frame defines the "*peripersonal space*", the space immediately surrounding our bodies (Previc, 1998). Within this space the subject can directly grasp and manipulate objects and tools. The subjects learn to interact with external objects in this frame using two different strategies (Newcombe & Huttenlocher, 2000):
   ▸ *Sensorimotor coding*: through the exact repetition of an acquired pattern of actions/movements;
   ▸ *Inertial navigation*: through the coding in terms of distance and direction from a starting position.

DOI: 10.1057/9781137431677.0006

▶ *Objective/far space* (body as object in a world*)*. It is shaped around the *"extrapersonal space"*, the space that occurs outside the reach of an individual (Previc, 1998). This space is defined by the spatial relations between the objects (*landmarks*) included in it: the subjects learn the position of the objects in this frame using two different strategies (Newcombe & Huttenlocher, 2000):
  ▶ *Cue learning*: remembering an object as located within a given area;
  ▶ *Place learning*: through the coding in terms of distance and direction from a landmark.

The extrapersonal space shapes the allocentric frame: within this frame the position of an object does not change if the subject moves, and the object exists even if there is no relation with the self or another person (Frith & de Vignemont, 2005). In this frame the body is an object like the other ones and its representation is the outcome of abstract knowledge, beliefs, and attitudes related to it as an object of third-person perception (looking at it from outside).

## Action, presence and the use of tools

We have seen that spatial perception is a dynamic operation that can be continuously modified and updated by the actions carried out by the subject. What happens when these actions are implemented using a tool?

According to the Merriam Webster's dictionary a "tool" is both "a handheld device that aids in accomplishing a task" and "something (as an instrument or apparatus) used in performing an operation" (Merriam-Webster, 2010). These definitions underline that tools are controlled by human action and that they exert an action upon external objects (Riva & Mantovani, 2012a,b, 2014). But, as reflected by the two different definitions, the relationship between the human action, the tool and its final effect is not always the same. For this reason, we can distinguish between two different types of mediated action (Riva & Mantovani, 2012b): first-order and second-order (see Figure 4.2).

In first-order mediated actions the subject uses the body to control a proximal tool (an artefact present and manipulable in the peripersonal space) to exert an action upon an external object. In practice, there is a

**First-order mediated action**
The subject uses the body to control a *proximal artefact* (the racquet) to achieve his/her intention (striking the ball).

**Second-order mediated action**
The subject uses the body to operate a *proximal artefact* (a joystick) that controls a different *distal artefact* (the avatar) to achieve his/her intention (to kick the adversary).

> **Learning to use the artefacts effectively and intuitively**

> **Learning to use the artefacts effectively and intuitively**

**Incorporation**
The proximal artefact extends the peripersonal space of the subject

**Incarnation**
The distal artefact extends the extrapersonal space of the subject

> **Spatio-temporal correspondence between multisensory feedbacks experienced by the user and the visual data related to the distal tool**

**Embodiment**
The user experiences a new body in the distal tool

**FIGURE 4.2**    *Taxonomy of the effects of presence using a tool*

direct spatial connection between the body of the subject, the tool and the external object. An example of first-order mediated action is the one of the tennis player striking the ball (external object) with the racquet (proximal tool).

In second-order mediated action the subject uses the body to control a proximal tool that controls a different distal one (a tool present and visible in the extrapersonal space) to exert an action upon an external object. In

DOI: 10.1057/9781137431677.0006

this situation there is a spatial disconnection between the peripersonal (near) space that contains both the body of the subject and the proximal tool, and the extrapersonal (far) space, that may be either real or virtual, where both the distal tool and the external object are located. An example of second-order mediated action is the one of the crane operator using a lever (proximal tool) to move a mechanical boom (distal tool in the real space) to lift materials (external real objects). Another example, more related to technology, is the one of the videogame player using a joystick (proximal tool) to move an avatar (distal tool in a virtual space) to pick up a sword (external virtual object). A possible, simpler variant of second-order mediated action is the direct use of the body to control a distal tool that exerts an action upon an external object. An example of this variant is the interaction with the Microsoft Kinect system: I move my body to move an avatar (distal tool) to pick up objects.

### Incorporation and incarnation

We suggest that these two mediated actions have different effects on our experience (Riva & Mantovani, 2014). A successfully learned first-order mediated action produces *incorporation*, in which the proximal tool extends the peripersonal space of the subject (the subject is present in the tool). A successfully learned second-order mediated action also produces *incarnation* in which a second peripersonal space is centred on the distal tool.

Since the seminal work of Atsushi Iriki on macaques (Iriki et al., 1996), many different studies demonstrated that, after a successful training, a proximal tool (first-order mediated action) is incorporated in the bodily experience of the subject (Farné et al., 2005; Farné et al., 2007; Hihara et al., 2006; Maravita & Iriki, 2004).

As explained by Maravita and Iriki (2004), "Recent neurophysiological, psychological and neuropsychological research suggests that this extended motor capability [the acquired ability of manipulating the tool] is followed by changes in specific neural networks that hold an updated map of body shape and posture (the putative 'Body Schema' of classical neurology). These changes are compatible with the notion of the inclusion of tools in the 'Body Schema', as if our own effector (for example the hand) were elongated to the tip of the tool" (p. 79).

In other words, the acquisition of a motor skill related to the use of a proximal tool extends the body model we use to define the near and

DOI: 10.1057/9781137431677.0006

far space. From a neuropsychological view point the tool is incorporated in our Body Schema, prolonging it till the end point of the tool. From a phenomenological viewpoint, instead, we are now present in the tool and we can use it intuitively as we use our hands and fingers.

But what happens when we learn to use a distal tool (second-order mediated action)? In a different experiment Iriki and colleagues trained macaques to retrieve food by watching their hand/arm movements through a real-time video monitor (Iriki et al., 2001). In other words, the monkey used the self-image in the monitor as a distal reference of hand movement, as happens using the Microsoft Kinect™. The study showed that the identical neurons, which code the image of the hand in normal condition, responded in a similar manner to the image in the video monitor: here, again, the image of the hand is experienced as a direct extension of the self. And this happened only after the acquisition of the new motor skill: before training no neuron responded to visual stimuli presented in the monitor screen. This requires an integration of the visual data (the distal tool) with the proprioceptive/tactile data (the real hand moving the proximal tool): How are they integrated?

Van Beers and colleagues (1996, 1999) suggest that our brain uses simultaneously the available visual and proprioceptive information to control the movement of the hand. Specifically, in cases of mismatches the role of the different data varies with direction (van Beers et al., 1999; van Beers et al., 2002): in azimuth (left-right), vision is more precise than proprioception; in-depth (near-far), however, proprioception is more precise than vision.

This suggests that second-order mediated action is based on the simultaneous handling of two different body models – one centred on the real body (based on proprioceptive data) and a second centred on the distal tool (visual data) – that are weighted in a way that minimizes uncertainty during the mediated action. This is in concordance with, for example, the work of Wirth and colleagues (2007) and Jäncke and colleagues (2009).

Interestingly, the passage between these models is not experienced as a possible breakdown. This is confirmed by the experimental data presented by Gamberini and Spagnolli (Gamberini & Spagnolli, 2003; Spagnolli & Gamberini, 2002). Describing the result of their analysis of 15 technical dysfunctions (e.g. to disentangle from the head mounted wires) experienced during the use of a virtual environment they conclude: "A sudden emersion from the virtual environment seems to

DOI: 10.1057/9781137431677.0006

be a rather inappropriate way to describe what happens. Participants remain focused on the navigation in the virtual environment, even though the environment they address with their actions is an expanded one" (Gamberini & Spagnolli, 2003, p. 1).

In second-order mediated actions the distal tool is the core of a second peripersonal space that extends the space of action and competes with the one centred on the body to drive action and experience. Specifically, when the distal-centred peripersonal space becomes the prevalent one, it also shifts the extrapersonal space to the one surrounding the distal tool. From an experiential viewpoint the outcome is simple: the subject experiences presence in the distal environment (telepresence). When a successfully learned second-order mediated action is implemented through an avatar this may, under certain conditions, produce *embodiment as the tool*, in which the user actually feels present as the avatar. We discuss this further in the next chapter (Chapter 5).

We can see now that presence makes possible the evolution of the Self through the incorporation of tools. Tools do not enable us only to extend our reaching space, but when successfully mastered they become part of a plastic neural representation of our body that allows their use without further cognitive effort (intuitively). In this way we can focus our cognitive resources on actions that are not only related to the here-and-now, thus improving the complexity of our goals (Damasio, 2010; Riva & Waterworth, 2003; Riva et al., 2004).

DOI: 10.1057/9781137431677.0006

# 5

# The Designed Presence of the Individual

**Abstract:** *Chapter 5 outlines how design affects the experience of presence for an individual acting and interacting in environments through the mediation of technology. The individual may experience mediated presence as a facet of being embodied in three different ways as a result of designed computer-mediation. In* expanded embodiment, *the individual experiences presence in a place that is not where his or her physical body is located – the designed-for effect of highly immersive virtual realities, real or fictional, wholly distinct from his or her current location. In contrast, in* altered embodiment, *the individual still experiences his or her current physical location in the physical world, but in a new way through the mediation of technology. This includes digital enhancement of both the physical environment and the body. Finally, the possibilities for designing new forms of individual presence are considered, around the notion of* distributed embodiment.

Waterworth, John and Giuseppe Riva. *Feeling Present in the Physical World and in Computer-Mediated Environments.* Basingstoke: Palgrave Macmillan, 2014. DOI: 10.1057/9781137431677.0007.

## Presence and embodiment

Presence reflects a central aspect of how an individual is embodied in an environment, whether this is the physical world, a virtual reality (VR), or a blended reality combining elements of both. As we have emphasized earlier, feeling highly present in a virtual reality is not essentially different from feeling highly present in the physical world. But the physical world is largely given as far as embodiment is concerned. We function in a world with certain characteristics, experienced normally through our evolved senses and other embodied capabilities and characteristics that underpin our sense of presence in the physical world. This is a product of evolution, not of design. However, our experience of the physical world is increasingly mediated by technology, and this tendency can only get stronger. So while the physical world is largely given – a world of solid objects and gravity – it is also mediated by technology. Public spaces and places such as airports, shopping centres, and sports arenas all include technology and all are designed, of course, as are restaurants, lifts, hospitals, and almost everywhere we find ourselves. However, the design of computer-mediated experiences within an augmented physical world (with given characteristics) is relatively new.

A sense of one's own presence can be seen as the yardstick of successful embodiment in a designed world. If you cannot feel really present, you are not embodied in the mediated world that has been created (as we have seen, one does not always feel very present, but the possibility must be there). In the rest of this chapter we consider design's role in facilitating three different categories of embodiment.

In *expanded embodiment*, the individual experiences presence in a place that is not where his or her physical body is located. This is the kind of "displaced" presence that can be produced by a convincing virtual reality environment, and it was this experience of feeling as if embodied in a different place, a place generated by computer, that initially stimulated interest in "telepresence", and then more generally in presence as experienced in different technologically mediated environments. The design possibilities of immersive virtual realities are enormous, but here we will focus on some different ways in which the individual's experience of presence in VR can be optimized.

Both the physical world and our own bodies are increasingly being augmented with digital technology that has the capacity to contribute to a designed sense of presence in the physical world, through *altered*

DOI: 10.1057/9781137431677.0007

*embodiment.* Here we will discuss some different design approaches for presence through altered embodiment, touching on digital enhancement of both the physical environment and the body. We will also stress the importance, when designing for presence in a mixed physical–virtual world, of considering the influence of varying contexts and communicational asymmetries between individuals.

Finally, we look at some of the possibilities for designing new forms of individual presence through what we have called *distributed embodiment* (Waterworth & Waterworth, 2014), representing quite fundamental changes to our experience of personal embodiment as generated through emerging ways of implementing computer-mediation of both the physical world and virtual reality.

## Expanded embodiment: displaced presence in virtual realities

Some degree of expanded embodiment accompanies mediated presence, as the term is commonly understood (Bracken & Skalski, 2010). This is most clear in a VR environment where the actual physical surroundings are shielded from the user as far as possible – to avoid distraction away from the virtual world. These distractions have been termed "breaks in presence" (Slater & Steed, 2000) but are actually shifts of presence from the virtual world to the physical world.

As with our sense of presence in the physical world, a first-person perspective is often a key ingredient in evoking strong presence in media. This is the norm in "classical" virtual reality, where we view the mediated world as if embodied there ourselves (to some degree) with normal senses and with a first-person perspective on things. We move our physical head and the virtual view changes accordingly; we move our physical arms and hands and we see a representation of these body parts depicted as if they were co-located with the internal image we have of our physical body. What is seldom implemented, however, is a realistic sense of locomotion in the virtual world that, as we described in Chapter 2, is a key factor in eliciting proto presence. When this proprioceptive layer of presence is not integrated with other layers, this will limit the experience of presence in the designed environment.

Expanded embodiment brings with it the possibility for presence in a mediated world, experienced as a more or less convincing perceptual

DOI: 10.1057/9781137431677.0007

"illusion of non-mediation" (Lombard & Ditton 1997). This might be a fictional world, such as an immersive VR game, or the convincing experience of being in another physical place – the original goal of telepresence (Minsky, 1980). Presence mediated in this way is the feeling of being embodied in a non-physically present external world, in the realization of which technology plays an active and direct role. The more the technology disappears from a person's attention and becomes experientially part of the self, the higher the level of presence through expanded embodiment. When this kind of VR realization is technically done well, there is no conflict between the mediated reality and the user's body schema or body image. It may even be possible to achieve higher levels of presence than are experienced in the physical world.

As already stated, we consider mediated presence to be basically an interactive perceptual illusion that depends on information being presented and entered in ways that – in some way – trigger a rich sense of embodiment in the mediated environment (Waterworth & Waterworth, 2003; Waterworth et al., 2010). It involves more than just perception and action, since high levels of presence cannot be maintained without intellectual and/or emotional engagement, but perception of an apparently real interactive environment surrounding the self is its core. Perception as a process results in hypotheses about what things exist in the immediate environment and what is happening (Gregory, 1997), which are then experienced as those things and events. Virtual reality, especially high quality and fully immersive VR with rich interactivity, fools the brain into perceiving that the body is somewhere it physically is not. This is why VR can have such powerful effects on the perceiver (Waterworth et al., 2010).

## Designing for maximal individual presence in VR

We suggested in Chapter 2 that presence should be considered as a layered experience, created through the evolution of the central nervous system in its attempt to embed the sensory-referred properties into an internal functional space. It therefore cannot be considered as just a simple response to media, with more immersion automatically eliciting higher levels of presence. Possible characteristics of high levels of presence come from recent researches into the concept of flow, which we briefly outline below. After that we describe some design aspects of situations that can lead to exceptional presence in mediated experiences.

DOI: 10.1057/9781137431677.0007

Csikszentmihalyi (1990, 1994) defined "flow" as an optimal state of consciousness characterized by a state of concentration so focused that it amounts to absolute absorption in an activity. According to Csikszentmihalyi (1977) when people are in a flow state "[they] shift into a common mode of experience when they become absorbed in their activity. This mode is characterized by a narrowing of the focus of awareness, so that irrelevant perceptions and thoughts are filtered out; by loss of self-consciousness; by a responsiveness to clear goals and unambiguous feedback; and by a sense of control over the environment ... it is this common flow experience that people adduce as the main reason for performing the activity" (p. 72).

Starting with this definition, different authors have tried to define flow in an operational way. For Ghani and Deshpande (1994) the two key characteristics of flow are (1) total concentration in an activity and (2) the enjoyment which one derives from an activity. Moreover, these authors identified two other factors affecting the experience of flow: a sense of control over one's environment and the level of challenge relative to a certain skill level. In Hoffman and Novak (1996), flow is defined in terms of the *experience* of flow (intrinsic enjoyment, loss of self-consciousness), behavioural properties of the flow activity (seamless sequence of responses and self-reinforcement), and its antecedents (skill–challenge balance, focused attention, and telepresence). If we compare these definitions with our three-layer model of presence, we can find many interesting similarities.

As described in Chapter 2, our three-layer, evolutionary model of presence suggests that maximal presence arises when proto consciousness, core consciousness and extended consciousness are focused on the same external situation or activity. Maximal presence thus results from the combination of all three layers with an abnormally tight focus on the same content (see Figure 5.1), so that attention is directed exclusively towards the current external situation. We suggest that this is compatible with the flow concept, and indicates one approach to designing mediated experiences of exceptional presence.

Normal, everyday levels of presence arise from a split of attentional resources between layers of differing content, with some attention being directed towards the current external situation. Minimal presence results from a lack of integration of the three layers, such that attention is mostly directed towards contents of extended consciousness that are unrelated

DOI: 10.1057/9781137431677.0007

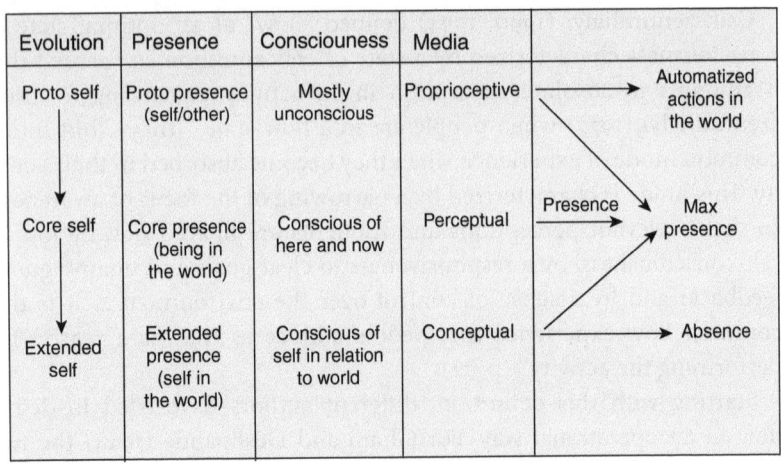

| Evolution | Presence | Consciouness | Media | |
|---|---|---|---|---|
| Proto self | Proto presence (self/other) | Mostly unconscious | Proprioceptive | Automatized actions in the world |
| Core self | Core presence (being in the world) | Conscious of here and now | Perceptual | Max presence |
| Extended self | Extended presence (self in the world) | Conscious of self in relation to world | Conceptual | Absence |

FIGURE 5.1    *Layers, media and mental states*
Source: from Riva et al. (2004).

to the present external environment – a psychological state of *absence* (Waterworth & Waterworth, 2001).

For us, maximal presence in a mediated experience arises from an optimal combination of form and content. The form must provide the means for a convincing perceptual illusion, but the content should be integrated with (and so attract attention to) the form for the illusion to happen convincingly. We suggest that proto presence is determined only by form, core presence by both form and content, and extended presence only by content. The integration of presence can occur in either the real or a virtual world. In the case of a virtual world, we need to provide both appropriate form and meaningful content. Presence in the real world depends only on content, on what we experience as happening to us in the here and now, since the form is provided and is always appropriate.

To maximize experienced presence in virtual environments we must design in a way that allows integration of the three layers (see Figure 5.1). As we have said, this is technically demanding at the lower levels. We need to provide as much immersion as possible, integrating proto (spatial) and core (sensory) presence. To integrate extended presence, the events and entities experienced in the virtual environment must have significance for the participant.

Maximal presence arises from an optimal combination of form and content. The form must provide the means for a convincing bodily and

DOI: 10.1057/9781137431677.0007

perceptual illusion, but the content should be integrated with (and so attract attention to) the form for the illusion of mediated presence to happen convincingly. We do not think we always feel presence when attending to something, internal or external, nor that the internal and external are always competitive in producing presence. On the contrary, the internal, "imaginal" content (of extended consciousness) may either enhance or detract from the overall sense of presence. An example of enhancement is a typical computer game, where game designers strive to ensure that content and form are well integrated. Optimal presence arises when the contents of extended consciousness are aligned with the other layers of the self, and attention is directed towards a currently present external world.

We can identify at least three ways of approaching the design of maximal mediated presence: *digital participation, mediated flow,* and *embodied immersion.* In these situations, the organism responds as if what happens in a mediated environment is real, in the fullest sense, and of immediate significance. Digital participation can arise if we design a role for the participant as a performer in an interactive drama (Nath, 2001) seen from a first-person perspective. If the performer becomes emotionally and intellectually engaged by the events in an appropriately immersive environment, extremely high levels of presence can be achieved (Waterworth et al., 2002). A feature of this state of participation is a corresponding loss of self-consciousness. Not that the self is not present – it is maximally so – but that an internal model of the self is not the focus of extended consciousness. In this respect, digital participation resembles the flow state – described above – during which extended consciousness is also not preoccupied with the idea of self.

Trevino and Webster were the first authors to study mediated flow. According to them (Trevino & Webster, 1992), this represents the extent to which (a) the user perceives a sense of control over the computer interaction, (b) the user perceives that his or her attention is focused on the interaction, (c) the user's curiosity is aroused during the interaction, and (d) the user finds the interaction intrinsically interesting. As with digital participation, events are experienced from a first-person perspective. Embodied immersion is our term for a style of interaction that uses bodily movements not only for consciously monitored control over the environment, as in standard computer interactions, but also for more direct, automatized inputs from the immersant. Pioneering artistic work in this area was carried out by Char Davies in the mid-1990s (see Davies,

DOI: 10.1057/9781137431677.0007

2003). In her Osmose, for example, breath and balance are used to control navigation, while in Ephémère visually dwelling on a portrayed "organic" form causes it to age before the eyes of the immersant. The work of Char Davies had an artistic purpose. In two more practical virtual environments, Relaxation Island and the Exploratorium, we developed virtual realities that responded to body states and movements as a way of changing mood, and learning to control one's own mood (Villani et al., 2005; Waterworth & Waterworth, 2004; Waterworth et al., 2004; Waterworth et al., 2003). As with the examples digital participation and mediated flow, this style of first-person mediated experience results in a loss of self-consciousness and, as with the others, we see this as an approach to eliciting maximal levels of presence.

Petranker (2003) distinguishes between "narratives", which are usually expressed in the third person and which we tell, or are told to us, and "stories", which we inhabit from a first-person perspective. For us, maximal presence arises when we fully "inhabit" the "story" of what is happening to us right now. Narrative, by its nature, is a distancing from the present. To design for maximal presence is to create stories we can inhabit as fully as possible. These stories are located in immersive environments and elicit embodied, unself-conscious and engaged participation from all three layers of the self.

## Altered embodiments: presence in mediated physical reality

In this section we consider ways in which the individual can experience a sense of presence, but in the physical world and via some form of computer-based mediation. We focus first on approaches to designing an intimately mixed reality, so-called *blended reality space* (Hoshi & Waterworth, 2009), where tangible physical objects and environmental displays are used to combine the physical and virtual smoothly and effectively, based on the design application of *blending theory* (Imaz & Benyon, 2006).

We also consider the reality of using technology while also active and mobile in the physical world. More and more, while travelling between, or simply functioning in various locations, we are also at the same time communicating with others located elsewhere. Not only do we feel social presence, as will be discussed in Chapter 6, we exist in a mixed reality

DOI: 10.1057/9781137431677.0007

where we experience social and individual presence simultaneously. Finally, we consider the fact that we can now use technological mediation to change the way our senses function, and indeed what senses we have. By designing new ways of perceiving the world we are effectively designing a new physical world around us.

## Designing presence in blended reality space

In an idealized form of computer-mediation of the physical world, the virtual and the physical would be smoothly mixed into a new combined form of reality – blended reality space (Hoshi & Waterworth, 2009). As a way of approaching this ideal, we have developed a design technique based on the notion of blends, as understood in the world of conceptual metaphor theory (Lakoff & Johnson, 1980; Falconnier & Turner, 2002). Designing with blends has been put forward as a general approach to interaction and software designing (Imaz & Benyon, 2006). We take this a step further by applying the approach to the designing of blended physical–virtual reality.

To illustrate what this means, consider the familiar desktop design of a typical personal computer – using windows, icons, menus and some means of pointing at virtual objects to select them (the so-called WIMP graphical user interface). At one time, this design was regarded as a metaphor based on a physical desktop, with its folders, documents, trashcan and so on. Interaction is by direct manipulation (via a mouse device) quite like moving and selecting objects, cutting and pasting text, in a physical office. However, recent users do not see the interface or style of interaction as being like working at a physical desk in an office. It is a PC interface, a thing in itself. "Cutting and pasting" means highlighting and moving text on a screen – the historical equivalent with scissors and glue is no longer relevant (except in the name). What has happened is that WIMP-based graphical user interfaces have become a blend rather than a metaphor, since the notion has become a new emergent space (Imaz & Benyon, 2006) – a thing in itself as far as cognition is concerned.

As an example, we can consider the process of blending applied to how we now understand a PC interface:

1   There are two input spaces, input space-1 and input space-2, and a cross-space mapping that connects elements and relations between the inputs. The two principal inputs have different organizing

DOI: 10.1057/9781137431677.0007

frames. Input space-1 refers to the frame of traditional computer operations, and input space-2 refers to the frame of office work.

2   A generic space maps onto each of the inputs and contains what the inputs have in common, which reflects some more abstract structure and organization shared by the inputs.

3   Blended conceptual space is an emergent conceptual structure with new ideas and insights. The emergent property of the blend provides direct manipulation and other features.

In the interfaces using the "desktop metaphor" with direct manipulation and access, the grasping, releasing, and opening of an object are imitated by dragging, dropping, and double clicking on perceivable icons, objects and folders on the virtual surface. But these are actually new emergent functions that exist neither in the real world nor in the technical domain of computer operations. They appear only in the blended conceptual space. Because of this newly emergent space, the experience is very distinctive from physical experience in everyday life, so that we experience a gap between the new blended space and our physical world of action. For example, as Imaz and Benyon (2006) also suggested, a computer window in the blended space is different from a real window and a menu on the space is different from a menu in a restaurant. Users experience a physical–virtual gap that disrupts the flow during activities that require a changeover between the physical and the virtual. They are forced into conscious effort to access information and carry out intentions (Hoshi & Waterworth, 2009).

In contrast, Figure 5.2 pictures a physical–virtual space that is immersive, interactive and body-movement oriented, and where there ideally need be little conscious effort of access to information. The user perceives and acts directly, as in everyday life activities, with the same potential for presence. We see the first examples of this form of altered embodiment in some commercial games such as Nintendo's Wii™ environment and some video-capture games (such as the Microsoft Kinect™) where the players have no direct physical connection with the game environment. Their physical movements are detected by either the "Wiimote" (the Wii remote control) or by a camera. Body movements performed by players are generally in response to game-initiated events. When their free body movements in physical space are tracked and used as inputs to the game, a truly merged physical/media space may be created during play, an example of *blended reality space* (Hoshi & Waterworth, 2009).

DOI: 10.1057/9781137431677.0007

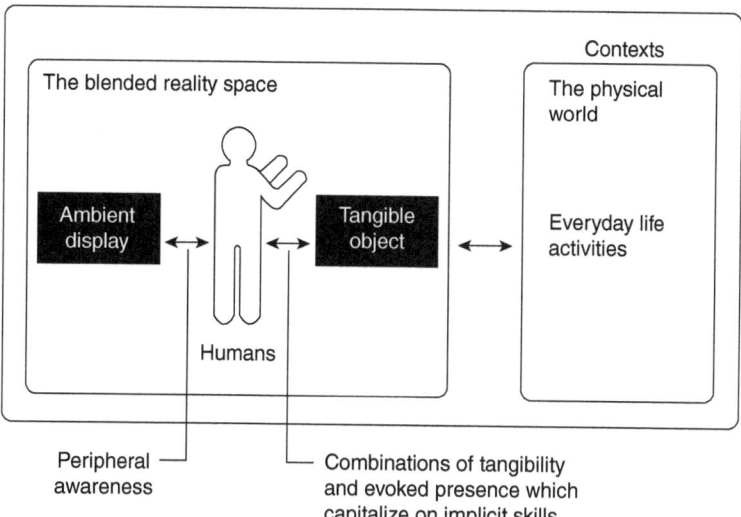

FIGURE 5.2 *Functioning within a blended reality space*
Source: from Hoshi and Waterworth (2009).

As information and communication technology becomes more pervasive in the built environment, such as video screens, electronic access systems and smart sensor techniques, the effectiveness of interactive mixed realities has been linked to the sense of presence as judged by users of the space (Bernardet et al., 2008). In blended reality space, peripheral display is combined with tangible interaction via objects whose physical characteristics reinforce the naturalness of their use (Hoshi & Waterworth, 2009).

The user of current tools such as mobile phones, computer applications, and medical devices needs to go through an early stage of learning to use a tool/device, performed with conscious attention (Kaptelinin & Nardi, 2006). In a Wii tennis situation, using a racket is the natural way of playing tennis, and the player has already become well-practiced and experienced without explicit user manuals or guidance. The physicality of the racket fills the gap between the physical and the virtual world. The conditions of weight, texture, and size of the racket, combined with sensor-based interaction techniques, help create a sense of presence in the blended reality space. The quality of actions and the strength of presence are correlated. The feeling of presence provides the player

DOI: 10.1057/9781137431677.0007

with feedback about the status of his or her activity within the situation in which the activity is carried out (the reader is referred back to the discussion of tool use in Chapter 4).

We suggest that optimal combinations of tangibility and peripheral displays carry the potential to make full use of, while not overburdening, the flexible but limited capacities of selective attention. This will be a key issue for the designing of future interaction approaches (Hoshi & Waterworth, 2009). Just as the user of a modern laptop is unaware of the historical reality of cutting and pasting with scissors and glue, so the individual in blended reality space will have little sense of what is virtual and what is physical.

## Appropriate presence in communicative contexts

By our view, cognitive load in a context where information is exchanged will tend to be inversely related to the level of presence experienced, since it is a reflection of the abstractness of a communicative medium that equates to internal (abstract) versus external (concrete) processing. However, as we suggested in Chapter 2, locus of attention is another important factor. While high cognitive loads will interfere more with other types of attentional task than low cognitive loads, two perceptual (and thus potentially presence-evoking) tasks will interfere with each other even though each imposes a relatively low cognitive load. In other words, presence cannot be viewed as a simple result of redundancy. A concrete, perceptual presentation of information – say an animation that portrays a simple narrative – will interfere less with other more abstract tasks than, say, a textual description. But if the individual is already focusing his or her attention on the external world, as when driving, there will be a conflict between the one perceptual task and the other.

The appropriate level of mediated presence in a specific context thus depends on both internal and external factors, not only on what the observer is thinking, but also on what she or he is perceiving and doing in the external world (or worlds). High presence requires and attracts a high level of attention, which may or may not be appropriate. For example, most mobile phone applications should not demand much attention, since the user is often engaged in other activities concurrently. In contrast, when one is separated from a loved one and wants to communicate richly, the highest possible level of presence may be preferred – by, for example, including sight, sound, tactile feedback, and perhaps even

DOI: 10.1057/9781137431677.0007

aroma. Thanks to the proliferation of mobile devices, a salient feature of modern communication patterns is their lack of symmetry. The different parties in a communication may be in different physical situations, each of which may have very different characteristics. They may be using different types of communication device.

In two completely different situations the same message could be interpreted very differently. As an example, imagine one person waiting for a flight, who receives a text message from a loved one as she is waiting. She has plenty of time to compose a heartfelt reply, but starts her message with a playfully provocative remark. As she is about to respond further, she hears an announcement to the effect that her flight is actually at a different gate, quite some way away. She realizes she will have move quickly to get to the gate in time. But she has no time to finish the conversation she has started, or even to explain her current urgent problem. Because she was expected to be in contact before catching the long flight, she sends the partially composed message and sets off for the correct gate. But the receiver, unaware of the context in which the message was composed, completely misunderstands the sender's intent and is upset by the tone of the communication.

This problem could be addressed in several ways. A communication medium with greater presence would make the problem less likely to arise. By definition, more presence evoked by a communication form means that more information about the present situation external to the sender is being transmitted. In a phone message, for example, the sender could explain the situation more quickly, while dashing to the correct location. And perhaps more importantly, the sender would also receive indications of the sender's true state, through paralinguistic cues such as breathing style, intonation, pitch and so on, as well as acoustic information from the surroundings. When video capability is also available, this tendency will be further enhanced, through the availability of facial expressions, visual features of the surroundings and so on.

A different approach would be to use sensor technology to monitor the sender's physiological state directly. Such information could be presented to the receiver in a variety of different forms, and transmitted as an annotation to any form of communication. Although the text message might be the same, the annotation would convey the fact that the sender was in an agitated state at the time the message was sent.

State-sensitive communication devices seem a promising way to cater for the fact that different individuals prefer and/or need different levels

DOI: 10.1057/9781137431677.0007

of presence in different situations. Contextual factors will also affect a person's state, and one of the most useful ways of tracking context may be through tracking the person's state, although without also tracking physical context this is open to misinterpretation and could be potentially hazardous.

## Presence with new, designed senses

In the preceding subsection we described how an appropriate design of the physical and virtual can support a sense of presence in a blended reality, thus allowing the individual access to the virtual world of information while still functioning in the physical world. Another way to support a sense of presence in a computer-mediated version of the physical world is by designing new sensory channels through which the physical world is experienced.

Don Ihde (1990) distinguished between an embodiment relation between a person and a technological artefact and a hermeneutic relation. In the former, the technology becomes embodied – as if part of the user's body – and perception is through the technology, which in itself is essentially transparent. In contrast, during the latter the user must interpret a more abstract representation of the information the technology provides. For us, Ihde's embodiment relation is a clear example of altered embodiment, which is characterized by a situation whereby my viewpoint is located in my physical body as normal, but I have changed perception, so that my sense of presence in the world around my body is potentially altered in some way and the technology mediates a world of which it is not perceived to be a part.

Altered embodiment is often an intended or unintended aspect of interacting with digital technology. Virtual reality can, in some circumstances, achieve a kind of "sensory rearrangement" resulting in modified experiences of one's own body (Biocca & Rolland, 1998; Castiello et al., 2004; Normand et al., 2011; Riva, 1998; Riva et al., 2011). In addition, altered embodiment can be seen as part of a general trend in the way many computer applications are designed: as perceptual tools, rather than cognitive artefacts (Norman, 1993). Waterworth (1997) refers to the potential of "synaesthetic media" – computer applications that provide an experience of information that is usually perceived in one form in a radically different form – to support enhanced creativity through new ways of perceiving information (see also Waterworth, 2003).

DOI: 10.1057/9781137431677.0007

When the idea of synaesthetic media is applied to a body functioning normally in the physical world, technology becomes a perceptual transducer producing a radically altered state of embodiment in the world. As an example, imagine how it would feel to have your senses altered by wearing the *Reality Helmet* (Waterworth & Fällman, 2003), a computerized system developed with the purpose of providing its users with the possibility of altered presence in physical reality. A custom-made helmet is combined with computational equipment placed in a custom built backpack to allow a high degree of mobility for its wearer. The eyes and ears are completely covered by the helmet. A digital video camera and stereo microphones are mounted on the outside of the helmet, while inside there are a pair of small visual displays and headphones. Through computer signal processing, the user's perceptual experience is transformed by providing a real-time visualization of the auditory environment in which the wearer is situated and an audio landscape of sound generated from digital video input. The user sees what he or she would normally hear, and hears what he or she would normally see. That the user feels present through this technological mediation is a reflection of his or her altered embodiment in the physical world.

Applications such as the Reality Helmet challenge the argument that degree of presence is a simple function of the level of subjective realism (see also Bouchard et al., 2012), at least in the normal sense of the word. A user trying to navigate the physical world while wearing the helmet will feel highly present (at least initially), because almost all available attention will be directed towards perceptual information. In altering the nature of embodiment, the form of the world we experience is also changed.

We naturally and unconsciously assume that the world has the form we normally perceive it to have, even though we may know that the senses we have are different from the senses other animals have, and that their perceptions of the world must be different from our own. This is not to say that the physical world does not exist, but its form is a matter of perception. Evolutionary adaptation results in forms of perception for particular types of organism (people, bats, cockroaches) that have tended to help them survive over many generations. Through the technical mediation that characterizes altered embodiment, we can now choose other forms (of perception and therefore of the world) that may help us to function in the rapidly changing mediated world we humans now inhabit. Or they may just be entertaining or artistically designed.

DOI: 10.1057/9781137431677.0007

There are many other examples of the related idea of *sensory substitution* (Bach-y-Rita & Kercel, 2003 is a well-known example), most commonly developed as assistive technology for those with some sensory disability such as blindness. "The voICe" (The voICe, 2014) is a recent system providing "augmented reality for the totally blind". Its main functionality is to convert video camera images into sound to enable the blind to navigate the world (and other information) by hearing instead of seeing.

When our embodiment is altered and we feel present in the physical world that surrounds the body, our perceptions of that world are radically changed. At the same time, when this is achieved to a high degree, we can experience a highly effective perceptual illusion of non-mediation (Lombard & Ditton, 1997), of presence, even though the world is dramatically changed for us relative to our everyday experience.

## Individual presence in other bodies

According to Metzinger (2006) there are three distinguishable aspects of human embodiment in the world. Like all animals, we are a body with certain physical characteristics and so have what Metzinger terms "first-order embodiment". And like all but the simplest animals, we also have associated and integrated perceptual motor systems that allow our bodies to function effectively in the world, often without the need for attention or even conscious supervision. This "body schema" comprises Metzinger's "second-order embodiment". The third order of embodiment is the "body image", the mental representation we have of our own bodies and which, it is said, few animals possess.

The sense of what is part of the self and what is not is actually quite flexible, and may be altered to extend beyond the reality of the biological body (e.g. Normand et al. 2009). Some technology can change the boundary of the body, by becoming perceptually part of the self – the blind man's stick is the classic example from phenomenology (Merleau-Ponty 1962) – when it is incorporated into the body schema. When this happens, it is as if the technology were functionally part of the body. When using the technology, it is as if the world starts where the tool ends. The technology is effectively part of the body during use, not of the world in which the body acts.

When we are aware of being in that external world and are not aware of the technology mediating our experience, this produces the feeling

DOI: 10.1057/9781137431677.0007

of presence through a perceptual illusion of non-mediation (Lombard & Ditton, 1997). Haans and IJsselsteijn (2012) consider third-order embodiment to be necessary for presence, but this is only the case when there is a conflict between the mediated view of the body and the body image of the perceiver. When this happens, the relevant mediating body extension becomes an object in the world rather than an integral part of the self. In contrast, in classic perceptual effects such as "the rubber hand illusion" (Botvinick & Cohen 1998), the mediated body part (the rubber hand) is integrated with the viewer's body image to dramatic effect. This and similar effects have been reproduced successfully in virtual reality and mixed reality situations (IJsselsteijn et al., 2006: Holmes & Spence, 2007, Slater et al., 2008).

## Distributed embodiment

Distributed embodiment goes beyond these cases, by separating the observer from the observed body. It is experientially very similar to naturally occurring out-of-the-body experiences (Blackmore, 1984). In these we may feel present, while at the same time observing our bodies from a "disembodied" viewpoint. These are relatively rare in nature, and poorly understood, so that they often connote something supernatural or mystical. The idea of distributed embodiment is stranger and harder to grasp than the other steps in interactive presence that we have discussed, because it is a contradictory state arising from conditions that – as far as the perceiving organism is concerned – should not be possible. But we are not referring here to the possibility to observe oneself as a controllable avatar in a virtual world, even though the characteristics of a represented avatar may have a significant effect on self-perception and behaviour (e.g. the Proteus Effect; Yee & Bailenson, 2007). Rather, distributed embodiment is the general case exemplified in the description of the third level of embodiment through tool-based action presented in Chapter 4 – embodiment as the tool.

It is already possible to produce the feeling of being in a virtual body that is also experienced as remotely located, separated from our own body. Simple technology has been used in this way to produce something similar to out-of the-body experiences for several years (e.g. Ehrsson, 2007; Lenggenhager et al., 2007, Petkova & Ehrsson, 2008). This is achieved by combining tactile and visual stimulation of the observer with corresponding and synchronized displays of the observed body

DOI: 10.1057/9781137431677.0007

apparently experiencing matching stimulation. As Petkova and Ehrsson report:

> Manipulation of the visual perspective, in combination with the receipt of correlated multi-sensory information from the body was sufficient to trigger the illusion that another person's body or an artificial body was one's own. This effect was so strong that people could experience being in another person's body when facing their own body and shaking hands with it. Our results are of fundamental importance because they identify the perceptual processes that produce the feeling of ownership of one's body. (2008, from the abstract)

This is a truly novel mode of consciousness for people in normal mental states, and opens up a wealth of new possibilities for entertainment experiences, in areas such as gaming, sports broadcasts and many other types of TV show. We can already, at least to some extent, produce the feeling of being in a virtual body that is also experienced as remotely located, separated from our own body. This is the feeling that "that is me over there, and I am present in that body". That body might look like this body, or not. If not, then it is as if I have different selves. If the other self looks like someone else, I might think that I have the experience of having their body – and I might have that experience, at least to some extent, as revealed in physiologic responses indicating appropriate emotional change (see New Scientist, 2010; Slater et al., 2010). This can be used in rehabilitation and for mediation between people, to change attitudes and increase empathy.

New, cheap, gaming technologies open these possibilities and more for everyday use. The most significant aspect of these new, inexpensive and modifiable systems is that they can readily and quite accurately locate and track several individual bodies, voices and faces in three-dimensional physical space. This means that, for example, an avatar or a robot can relatively easily be programmed to mirror the movements and facial expressions of a person, either locally or at a distance. This might lead to developments such as:

▶ teleconferencing applications, where the participants are represented as avatars that move their bodies and faces in exact accord with those of the distributed participants;
▶ wall-sized responsive displays, controlled by the body and in almost any location;
▶ interactive "fitting rooms" for trying on new clothes before buying;

DOI: 10.1057/9781137431677.0007

▶ remote control of (as) robots;
▶ interactive "workbenches" and other surfaces for close, highly dexterous interaction (architecture, inspecting medical imagery);
▶ physiotherapeutic application and sports training.

The other is not confined to human bodies. With the right visual and tactile stimulation, one could in principle feel present in an animal body, or even an inanimate object. If I see myself as that creature or thing, and feel myself to be present in that body, might I come to know what it feels like to be, for example, a bat (Nagel, 1974) or a box? This is more than virtualization, more than the representation of things and its behaviour, and my ability to identify with them. It is the feeling that I am present as them – not metaphorically, literally.

Presence transference to another body – distributed embodiment – need not involve much simulation. All of this can be accomplished through virtual reality, where every pixel and all behavioural and physical responses must be specified precisely to cover all possible events. But it can also, and more easily and flexibly, be done in the augmented reality we increasingly inhabit. This includes sensors in objects, people and even animals, and distributed large and small displays that respond to sensed events nearby or at a distance. This reality mixes the real and the virtual in a blended world of almost unimaginable possibilities.

## Future ways of being present: challenges and possibilities

Many existing computing applications can be viewed as synaesthetic media; they are too numerous and too familiar to be reviewed in detail here. Obvious examples include programs that take an input – such as a stream of music – and turn it into an output in another form – such as a dynamic visual display of the amplitude of various frequency bands. Almost any computer-produced visualization, sonification, haptic or other display that present information through a realization form other than the original can be seen as a synaesthetic medium. But most of these do not provide altered embodiment, because the experience is not integrated with that of the surrounding environment.

Only when computer-based information is blended with the perception of the surrounding physical world is there the potential for a new form of altered embodiment. That requires that the augmentation of the physical with the virtual be carried out in such a way that the user has the ability to feel present. Given the clear popularity of mobility and

DOI: 10.1057/9781137431677.0007

social connectivity, presence will probably be experienced increasingly through attention to a blended external world (see also Benyon, 2012; Google Glass, 2013; Hoshi et al., 2011). For this to work in practice, a major challenge will be to make media devices sensitive to the situational context of their use, and the state of their users. Presence levels could then in principle be dynamically adjustable to maintain optimal functioning in an unfolding blended reality stream.

The design space of sensory transformations with technology is huge, which not only provides enormous potential but is also highly challenging for designers. We can see that altered embodiment opens up a new way of being in a world, and of experiencing presence. Indeed, it changes not only the body but also the perceived form of the physical world in which the body is located. In designing altered embodiment, the possibilities are almost endless – but we do not yet know much about what will work best for which purpose, or about possible longer-term effects on the perceiver.

Many convincing demonstrations of expanded embodiment already exist, for example, in psychotherapy, entertainment, training, and mental and physical rehabilitation. The power of expanded embodiment as produced by well-designed immersive VR applications is already well-known, and several of these are treated in detail elsewhere in this volume. New design possibilities are opened up when already successful approaches to eliciting expanded embodiment are combined with the huge, but relatively untapped, potential of altered embodiment.

Design challenges of distributed embodiment include specifying the means of being in other bodies, of switching between bodies, and the characteristics of those bodies – which could include human (self or not, lifelike or not), robotic, animal (Nagel, 1974), or even inanimate objects (Misselhorn, 2009). It is unlikely that all these possibilities will be effective in practice. Distributed embodiment can be accomplished in virtual reality, but it can also – at least in principle – be implemented in the blended reality of the physical and the virtual that is increasingly our everyday habitat. With appropriately placed cameras and other sensors, as well as mobile and ambient displays, physically close and distant people will interact through context-sensitive applications producing – as appropriate – altered, expanded and distributed embodiment. The design possibilities, and challenges, are enormous.

Our changing experiences of presence reflect the changing virtual–physical world in which we live. The blending we refer to in this chapter

DOI: 10.1057/9781137431677.0007

also implies the combination, through the mediation of technology, of a wide range of experiences – many of which will involve communication with others. The differences and similarities between the experience of individual and that of social presence, and how these two types of presence experience relate to each other, are the subject of the next chapter (Chapter 6).

DOI: 10.1057/9781137431677.0007

# 6

# Presence in Social Environments

**Abstract:** *Chapter 6 focuses on the applications of presence in social computer-mediated environments, considering the importance of distinguishing social from individual presence. In individual presence the agent pre-reflexively controls his/her action, whereas during social presence the agent pre-reflexively recognizes and evaluates the action of others. The strength of feeling of social presence is determined by two factors: the extent to which conscious attention is tightly focused or more diffuse, and the degree of integration of three different layers. In this case the three layers are (i) Imitative Social Presence (there is an intentional Other like the Self), (ii) Interactive Social Presence (the intention of the Other is towards the Self), and (iii) Empathic Social Presence (the Self and the Other share the same intention). Maximum social presence produces what is called "group flow" and is a key to understanding the creativity of groups in collaborative settings.*

Waterworth, John and Giuseppe Riva. *Feeling Present in the Physical World and in Computer-Mediated Environments.* Basingstoke: Palgrave Macmillan, 2014. DOI: 10.1057/9781137431677.0008.

# Social presence

As we have seen previously, the concept of presence concerns the subject and his or her ability to act in the world: I am present in a real or virtual space if I am able to put my intentions into action. But how does one connect to others? How do others become present for the subject? To answer these questions we return to the recent discovery of "mirror neurons" previously introduced in Chapter 3. These neurons, discovered to be in the ventral pre-motor cortex of apes (area F5), have amongst other qualities that of becoming activated when an animal performs a given action, as we saw. But they are also activated in the same way when one animal sees another animal – man or ape – performing the same action (Rizzolatti et al., 1996; Rizzolatti & Sinigaglia, 2006). In this way, the individual who observes another is able to put himself in the shoes of the actor, to understand what another is doing, intuitively, because the same neuronal activity is taking place.

The result is the creation of neural representations which are shared on two levels (Gallagher & Jeannerod, 2002):

▸ On the one hand, execution and observation share the same neural substratum in one individual subject;
▸ On the other, when a subject observes another subject's action, the same representations are simultaneously active in the brains of both subjects.

This means that at neural level, the action performed and the action observed are codified in a multi-subjective format, which does not recognize actor or observer. This process is only effective if the subject is capable of distinguishing between an action performed and an action perceived. As Becchio and Bertone (2005) point out: "By codifying an agent-free representation of action, mirror neurons support the visual and motor comprehension of the action, but are not in themselves enough to attribute an action to an agent. This level of comprehension, defined as agentive by the authors, requires that the agent parameter is specified as a separate parameter: only in this way does the action become the action of a particular agent" (p. 859).

As discussed in Chapter 2, presence is the facility that allows a subject to distinguish between himself or herself and another. In presence, "an I and an Other are created". The "Other similar to the Self" is a variation of one of the two relevant elements (Self and Other) that the organism

DOI: 10.1057/9781137431677.0008

is able to identify within its perceptive flow. This suggests the existence of a second selective and adaptive mechanism, "social presence", which enables the Self to identify and interact with the Other by understanding the Other's intentions. From an evolutionary point of view, social presence has three functions:

1  To enable the subject to identify the Other and to attribute to him an ontological status – "the Other similar to the Self" – different from other objects perceived.
2  To allow interaction and communication through the understanding of the Other's intentions. From the computational viewpoint, it is essentially the same approach used in presence (Figure 5.1):
   ▸ First, the agent recognizes a motor intention, and identifies the actor as another intentional Self (Other);
   ▸ Second, an efference copy of the motor command is fed to a forward dynamic model that generates a prediction of the consequences of performing this motor command (goal);
   ▸ Third, the predicted state is compared with the actual sensory feedback. Errors derived from the difference between the predicted state and the actual state (break) can be used to update the model and improve performance.
3  To permit the evolution of the Self through the identification of "optimal shared experiences" and the incorporation of artefacts – physical and social – linked to them.

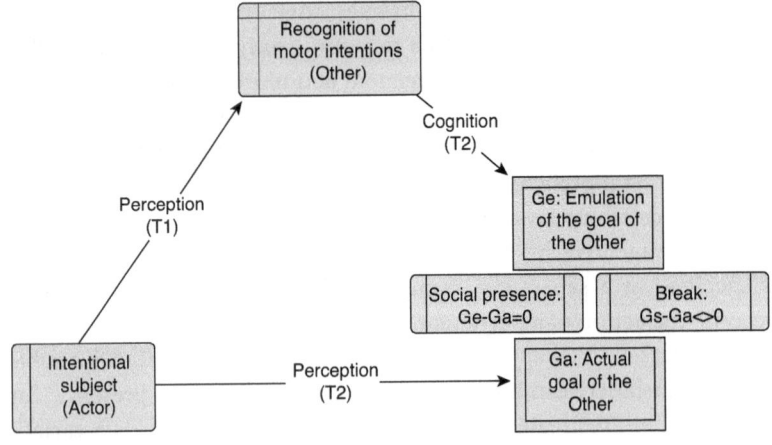

FIGURE 6.1    *The experience of social presence*

DOI: 10.1057/9781137431677.0008

In summary, we can define social presence (Biocca et al., 2003; Gaggioli et al., 2013; Riva, 2008; Riva et al., 2003; Riva & Mantovani, 2014) as the sensation of "being with other Selves" in a real or virtual environment, resulting from the ability to intuitively recognize the intentions of others in our surroundings.

## The evolutionary role of social presence

From the combined analysis of presence and social presence, it emerges that the point of contact between these two processes clearly lies in intentions and their codification by means of motor representations of action (Knoblich & Flach, 2003; Prinz, 1997):

▸ Presence verifies the effective fulfilment (enaction) of the intention in action.
▸ Social presence permits the identification of the Other's intentions through the analysis of his actions.

We have also seen in Chapter 3 how the dynamic theory of intentions describes an intention as a dynamic structure organized on three levels. In the following section we will see how this triadic structure can be attributed to the evolutionary process of the Self and is also existent in social presence.

### The three levels of social presence

The importance of imitation in developmental psychology and in particular its link to empathy and intentionality have driven several researchers to explore this area of study. Andrew Meltzoff's research is well-known in developmental psychology for having demonstrated that, unlike Piaget suggested, a child is capable of imitating various gestures made by an adult – sticking out their tongue, opening their mouth or moving a finger – as early as two or three weeks old (Meltzoff & Moore, 1977). Meltzoff and Decety recently summed up 25 years of research on imitation in a review for the Royal Society (Meltzoff & Decety, 2003). The article identifies three phases in the development of imitative skills:

1  *The capacity to imitate a human being*: as we have noted, the child begins to develop this capacity when it is two weeks old. During

DOI: 10.1057/9781137431677.0008

this phase, the child learns first which parts of the body to move and how to move them.

2  *The capacity to identify a human being who is imitating the child*: the child begins to develop this ability at around 14 months. The child understands that, although he is not controlling the adult's actions, the adult is imitating him.

3  *The capacity to recognize intentions and emotions in a human being*: from 18 months the child is able to understand that a subject's activities are structured in terms of objectives and intentions.

On the basis of these points, Meltzoff has developed the "like me" model, which explains the structure of the process in three successive phases through which a child is able to develop a theory of the mind (Meltzoff, 2007):

1  *The presence of an innate predisposition for action representation*: thanks to mirror neurons the child is able to experience a perceived action almost as if he had performed it.

2  *First person experience*: through his daily experiences the child learns to connect his motor acts with mental states. For example, the child learns to connect the feeling of having a wish being denied with the facial expressions and movements that indicate this.

3  *Understanding other minds*: when the child sees other people behaving like him, he is able to understand that, by analogy, they are experiencing the same mental state as he does when he behaves that way.

This suggests that social presence includes three different layers/subprocesses that are phylogenetically different, but mutually inclusive (Riva & Mantovani, 2012, 2014):

▸ Other's Presence (Other vs the Self–M-intentions);
▸ Interactive Presence (Other towards the Self – P-intentions);
▸ Shared Presence (Other is like the Self–D-intentions).

The first level of imitative skills – the ability to imitate a human being – corresponds to "Other's Presence", the ability to recognize motor intentions, which allows the Self to recognize an intentional Other. The better the subject is able to *recognize within the sensorial flow the stimuli which relate to* "another similar to the Self", the better he is able to carry out an intention, and thus increase his chances of survival (the Other in opposition to the Self).

DOI: 10.1057/9781137431677.0008

The second level of imitative skills – the ability to identify a human being who is imitating me – corresponds to "Interactive Presence", the ability to recognize motor and proximal intentions which allows the Self to identify the Other whose intention is directed towards him. The better the subject is able to *recognize within the sensorial flow the intention direct towards him by* "an Other similar to the Self", the greater the chances of successfully carrying out an action, and therefore the greater the chances of survival (the Other towards the Self).

The third level of imitative skills – the ability to recognize the intentions and emotions of a human being – corresponds to "Shared Presence", the ability to recognize motor, proximal and distal intentions, which enables the Self to identify another whose intentions correspond to his own. The better the subject is able to *recognize within the sensorial flow an* "Other similar to the Self" *with intentions the same as his own,* the better he will be able to successfully initiate collaborative interaction or communication, increasing his chances of survival (the Other like the Self).

Shared Presence permits the subject to feel empathy, *the capacity to see oneself in another person, to get inside another's thoughts and state of mind.* During the experience of empathy, the subject separates himself/herself from his own intentional and emotional state, and identifies with that of another person (the Other merges with the Self).

As with individual presence, the three levels are evolutionarily organized: from the lowest to the highest. However, unlike with individual presence, the levels of social presence are not functionally separate but mutually inclusive. This leads to two consequences. The superior levels also include the inferior levels: if the subject is able to understand distal intentions (Shared Presence), he is also capable of understanding motor intentions (Other's Presence). At the same time, it is impossible to activate the higher levels of social presence if the lower levels are not activated first. If I am unable to understand a subject's proximal intentions (Interactive Presence) then I will not be able to understand his distal intentions (Shared Presence).

The three levels of social presence are linked by *simultaneous influences on the subject's capacity for social interaction.* The way in which the interaction is experienced changes depending on the level of social presence experienced by the subject. It is important to note that, as with presence, the subject is unaware of the role of social presence in determining the characteristics of his actions. He is, however, evolutionarily programmed to perceive the shift from one level of social presence to another in social

DOI: 10.1057/9781137431677.0008

interactions. Furthermore, if this shift offers a valuable opportunity, the subject can act to increase his level of social presence. For example, if a girl starts staring at me at a party, I immediately become aware of the shift from Other's Presence (the girl is at the same party as me) to Interactive Presence (the girl is looking at me). If the girl is interesting, I can approach her and talk to her in order to understand her intentions. Is she looking at me because she likes me or because I have a stain on my jacket?

## The social process: the point of contact between presence and social presence

So far we have analysed presence and social presence separately, but there is a very strong link between them: the social process. It is because of presence and social presence that it is possible to communicate. To be able to communicate the two parties, as well as sharing a set of common concepts, must be able to recognize the presence of another in the same situation (Other's Presence), understand the Other's wish to begin communication (Interactive Presence), identify the intention which the Other expresses through communication (core presence and extended presence) and express their own actions through motor acts (proto presence).

The relationship between social process and presence is bidirectional. Presence and social presence are necessary in order to interact and communicate and it is through the social process that the subject and the group evolve. When this happens, the subjects and the group progressively increase both the characteristics of their own intentions (from motor to distal) and the sense of presence that they experience, creating the basis for new creative acts, both individual and group.

## Presence, activity and optimal experiences

One of the deductions that can be made from what has been discussed so far is the existence of a link between presence and the effectiveness of an action. The greater level of presence a subject experiences in an activity, the greater the organism's involvement in the activity will be, and this increases the probability of the activity ending well (the transformation of the intention into action). This is particularly important when the

DOI: 10.1057/9781137431677.0008

subject carries out the activity by using a tool, including media. The use of a tool compels the subject to modify his action, forcing him to adapt himself to the tool. In this case, given equal conditions and skills, the greater efficacy of the activity when carried out using a tool is linked to the tool's ability to facilitate the subject in increasing his level of presence. We give an example to explain this below.

Imagine that we have a computer and want to copy a file from a disk onto a USB stick. We have seen that proto presence constitutes the first level of presence, which concerns the level of coupling between movement and perception. This means that an activity in which it is easy to immediately identify the result of one's own movements is preferable to an activity in which this is not possible or not easy. For this reason the subject, all things being equal, will tend to choose a method which facilitates the direct perception of movement (I move the file by dragging it with the mouse) as opposed to one which does not (typing the instruction "copy name-of-file a: b:"). Likewise, using the arrow key on the keyboard to copy the file is preferable to using an instruction, but worse than using the mouse.

During an activity we are obviously not influenced by only one level of presence, but by all three levels working together. For example, when we are doing a distance-learning training course, interaction with the mouse is preferred to interaction with the keyboard (proto presence); the use of multimedia equipment is better than making use of a simple text (core presence); undertaking tasks linked to experience and to the interests of the project is preferable to carrying out abstract tasks (extended presence). But what happens when we have to choose between activities or artefacts that differ between the different levels of presence? For example, how do users choose between a distance-learning training course with interesting modules but which uses only texts, and another which makes extensive use of multimedia but which addresses less interesting topics? In these situations, the level of presence that is evolutionarily superior prevails: first extended presence, followed by core and then proto presence. Users will generally choose the course featuring interesting topics but which only uses text.

A second consequence of the considerations discussed in Chapter 5 is the existence of certain "optimal experiences" in which the individual experiences the maximum feeling of presence at each of the three levels. This experience, when it is associated with a positive emotional state, is defined as a "flow experience" (Csikszentmihalyi, 1990, 1994). This state

DOI: 10.1057/9781137431677.0008

is characterized by a high level of concentration and participation in the activity, by the balance of the perception of the difficulties of the situation and the challenge with personal skills, by the distortion of the sense of time (the internal clock slows down, whilst the external one speeds up), and by a natural interest in the process which produces a sense of pleasure and satisfaction.

Similar considerations also apply to social presence. First, there is a link between presence and efficacy of interaction: the more often the organism experiences a high level of social presence during interaction, the greater his ability to understand the Other, and therefore the chances of the interaction being successful increase.

Second, there is also a specific optimal experience for social presence, "networked flow", which is the result of the association between

▸ *maximal levels of social presence*: the feeling of sharing objectives and emotions with others;
▸ *group members' perception of being in a phase of liminality*: a state of transition, of being "about to ...", in which the earlier positive condition is no longer present, and the future positive condition has not yet come into being;
▸ *shared recognition of a possible common strategy for exiting from liminality*: everybody working towards a shared objective, which the group can change;
▸ *maximal levels of individual presence*: the feeling of being able, through personal involvement in the group, to successfully transform intentions into actions.

The term "liminality" above denotes a state of transition, of being "about to ...", in which an earlier positive condition is no longer present, and a future positive condition has not yet come into being (Turner, 1982). A typical situation of liminality is when a recent graduate is looking for work: he is no longer a student, but he is not yet employed. When this happens the subject is naturally pushed towards change. His situation is linked to the psychological concept of the "inner conflict", described by Festinger (1957) and by Miller and Rollnik (1991) as the perception of a discrepancy between reality on one side, and aspirations and expectations on the other. Inner conflict pushes the subject to change, but the effectiveness of the change is linked to the self-efficacy of the subject, in the subject's belief in his ability to change his own behaviour (Bandura, 1997). If the subject

DOI: 10.1057/9781137431677.0008

thinks that he is able to change, he will try to do so. If not, he will wait until he is forced to do so by a feeling of uneasiness or by his surrounding environment.

A maximal level of social presence permits the subject to increase their self-efficacy and to find the motor for change within shared group activity. Specifically, the sensation of sharing objectives and ideals, associated with the push for change brought about by the feeling of liminality, can lead the group to an experience of networked flow (Gaggioli et al., in press; Gaggioli et al., 2011; Gaggioli et al., 2013).

## The result of optimal experiences: memes

Gaggioli and colleagues (Gaggioli et al., in press; Gaggioli et al., 2011, 2013) recently suggested that during an optimal experience the subject is able to produce creative works more easily. Notably, optimal experiences are fundamental for the creation and diffusion of "memes". The concept of a meme was first introduced by the zoologist Richard Dawkins, comparable to the concept of the gene: an element of culture which can be transmitted from one individual to another by non-genetic means, and in particular through imitation (Blakemore, 1999; Dawkins, 1989). Dawkins presents the concept of memes as part of the theory of "universal Darwinism", according to which life evolves through the differential survival of self-replicating entities – "replicators".

If a gene is a replicator of a particular genotype, a meme is the replicator of a phenotype (Dawkins, 1989): a unit of cultural information which is copied with variations or errors, and whose nature influences its chances of replication. In practice, it is via memes that skills, habits or manners are transmitted from one person to another through imitation. For this reason, memes do not correspond to cultural units, but are selected by them (ibid.). There are three elements in Dawkins's definition which were not sufficiently explained by Dawkins (Blakemore, 1999; Distin, 2005):

▸ The content of the meme, or, more specifically, what type of cultural information it contains.
▸ The different ways in which memes can be transmitted.
▸ Whether memes only exist inside the brain or do they exist outside too?

DOI: 10.1057/9781137431677.0008

According to Gaggioli and colleagues (2013) the memes' content is intentional: each meme contains within it a specific intention. Furthermore, the creation and diffusion of memes depend on the level of presence and social presence experienced during action and communication. Specifically:

▸ *Memes are more likely to be created during an activity characterized by high levels of presence:*
   ▸ The condition required for the creation of a meme is a high level of extended presence, that is, the intention must contain elements of particular significance for the subject's representations. For example, if I am sitting in my armchair listening to a song on the radio that brings to mind memories from my past, then the words and notes will tend to become fixed in my memory.
   ▸ Moreover, high levels of proto and nuclear presence linked to extended presence further increase the chances of creating memes. The more vivid the music is, the greater the possibility that a meme will become activated.
   ▸ The concept of presence allows us to predict the development of memes, even in situations where there is a high level of extended presence but a negative emotional element. For example, the screams of a hunter engaged in combat with a wild beast may become a meme and be used by other hunters to indicate the moment of battle.
▸ *Memes are more easily replicated during an activity characterized by high levels of presence and social presence. The replication of memes requires:*
   ▸ *High levels of extended presence*: the interaction must contain notable significant elements for the subject's representations.
   ▸ *High levels of Shared Presence*: during the intentional interaction I must be able to understand the meaning that the "Other similar to myself" attaches to it.
   ▸ When the meme is produced by a "friend" – a person who I consider like myself, or by a person who I respect – and during an activity directed towards an objective which is important to me, the probability of the meme being transmitted (the internalization of the intention) increases significantly. This explains why the behaviour of singers and actors is so often imitated by their fans.

DOI: 10.1057/9781137431677.0008

# From the group to society: the role of narration

The creation of a new meme – a new product, a new concept, a new style – does not necessarily imply its diffusion. As we have seen, the transmission of memes is strongly linked to the level of social presence experienced during the interaction between the subject who passes on the meme, and the subject who receives it. There is, however, a tool that is able to facilitate this process: narration. As noted by Bruner (1991): "Just as our experience of the natural world tends to imitate the categories of familiar science, so our experience of human affairs comes to take the form of the narratives we use in talking about them" (p. 5).

It is narration that connects one meme to another, giving them a sense and allowing people outside the group to recognize them as possible intentions (internalization). The link between narrative, memes, individuals, society and activities, exists on four levels:

1  *Individual*: narrative thought is the cognitive tool which enables us to interpret situations and to construct a vision of the world which is not only related to the present but also guides our individual activities.

2  *Social*: narratives allow memes to connect with each other, so that the community of customs could be defined. This allows social activities to be structured and artefacts to be constructed.

3  *From social to individual*: through the processes of positioning and internalization, narratives influence the characteristics of our social identity and our vision of the world.

4  *From individual to social*: through narration, made possible by narrative thought and the process of externalization, we are able to share our vision, expressed in a series of memes, which allows common activities in the community of customs to be structured.

Narrative psychology maintains that a significant part of knowledge of the Self is organized in narrative schemes which the individual uses to interpret reality and to give it meaning (Crossley, 2000; Rollo, 2007). Hutto, exponent of the Narrative Practice Hypothesis (2008), is one of the foremost advocates of this view and he defines the narrative structures which facilitate social interpretation as "folk psychology narratives": narratives which allow the listener or reader to understand the thoughts, actions and feelings of the characters. These narratives are structured not as rules but as descriptions of subjects who act according

DOI: 10.1057/9781137431677.0008

to precise objectives and whose actions change their emotional state and their relationship with the world.

As Hutto (2008) notes, the most effective conversations are those in which the subject is forced to present and negotiate his personal point of view. Using the same terminology that we have employed thus far, it can be said that only narratives in which the subject is present are able to position the subject: the greater the subject's presence, the greater the positioning effects of the narrative.

DOI: 10.1057/9781137431677.0008

# 7
# Conclusions

Abstract: *The book concludes with a summing up of our theoretical perspective on presence and of how a consideration of when and why we feel present can help us to understand our relationship with and experience of the world, and especially of the computer-mediated environments in which we increasingly live our daily lives. Brief speculations are also made about the ways in which presence will develop in the future, both in immersive virtual realities and in evolving blends of the physical and the virtual.*

Waterworth, John and Giuseppe Riva. *Feeling Present in the Physical World and in Computer-Mediated Environments.* Basingstoke: Palgrave Macmillan, 2014. DOI: 10.1057/9781137431677.0009.

## Summing up

This book focuses on our ability to feel present in physical and computer-mediated environments: on what this sense of presence is, how it developed, and why it matters. We have suggested that the sense of presence is a basic mental faculty designed by evolution to ensure that organisms know when they are attending to things in their here and now that might affect their survival. It allows people to distinguish internally imagined events from actually present external events.

Although presence is a basic and necessary capacity with a long evolutionary history, interest in presence is relatively new, and came to the fore with the advent of virtual reality in the 1980s and 1990s. While people have always felt more or less present in the physical world, having a comparable experience in a computer-generated environment was surprising and in need of explanation. When the body is coupled dynamically to the way information is experienced, as in an immersive virtual reality, convincing experiences of presence in the portrayed reality are produced and these affect the immersant physically, emotionally, cognitively and even, sometimes and with appropriate design, spiritually or philosophically.

In this book, we have emphasized the view that the sense of presence is a basic mental faculty designed by evolution to ensure that organisms know when they are attending to things in their here and now that might affect their survival. And that to do this, they need to *feel directly* when they are attending to the current external world in which they are present, and that this is the feeling of presence. In a convincing virtual reality, this mechanism is fooled by the way the technology mimics and caters to how we naturally perceive the world.

Feeling present in a computer-mediated world is essentially no different from feeling present in the physical world, though it is only in recent years that it has been possible to reach high levels of mediated presence. By this view, the design of effective presence-inducing digital worlds should be based, to a far greater extent than most developers realize, on what we know about the ways in which our brains process incoming sensory signals (see also Gallace & colleagues, 2012). What is needed is an approach that can be defined as "neurally inspired" simulation, rather than one based on the attempt to reproduce the characteristics of physical stimuli ("external world" simulations).

Presence is a key link between intention and action, bridging the gap that otherwise exists between existing accounts based on purely

DOI: 10.1057/9781137431677.0009

cognitive or volitional perspectives. A key difference between digital and non-digital tools is that in designing the former the world on which and in which the tool acts is also modified. We developed this notion further by tracking the development of presence through the ways in which digital tools may be used to enact our intentions, from *incorporation* of the tool, through *incarnation* via the tool, and towards *embodiment* as the tool itself. From this "neurally inspired" perspective, the sense of presence provides a measurable yardstick of successful embodiment in a designed world.

We have outlined several approaches to the design of mediated presence yielding distinctive modes of embodiment. In *expanded embodiment*, the individual experiences presence in a place that is not where his or her physical body is located. The experience is designed to replace, as completely as possible, a person's perception of being in his or her actual physical location. We also described ways in which this effect can be maximized in the design of virtual realities. By our account, the strength of feeling present is determined by two main factors: the extent to which conscious attention is tightly focused or more diffuse, and the degree of integration of different layers of presence derived from three levels of the functioning of the self: proto (proprioceptive) presence, core (perceptual) presence, and extended (reflective) presence.

Maximum presence occurs when attention is tightly focused, and the three layers are integrated. Absence occurs when attention is tightly focused but the three layers are not integrated. Failures or maladjustments of the presence ability have predictable consequences in various forms of psychological distress that can be understood in terms of our model. Our view is that it is from the experienced distinction between presence and absence that the therapeutic potential of new information technology derives.

In contrast to presence in virtual reality, *altered embodiment* is a result of the fact that both the physical world and our own bodies are increasingly being augmented with digital technology that has the capacity to contribute to a designed sense of presence in a computer-mediated version of the actual physical world. This may be achieved through the implementation of altered or new senses for the person acting in the world. It may also be achieved by blending the physical and the virtual, through the use of wearable and embedded technology incorporating location-awareness and other sensors, as well as mobile, wearable and ambient displays. *Distributed embodiment* separates the observer from

DOI: 10.1057/9781137431677.0009

the observed body. In this case, the actor is embodied as the tool itself – which may be represented as an avatar of the user, another person, or something entirely different. The possible development and application of such an approach is as yet unclear.

The focusing of the layers of consciousness that underlies maximal presence represents the self in actions that effectively realize its intentions in its external environment – physical or computer-mediated. This state of maximal presence also implies a loss of self-consciousness, since attention given to the idea of self that underlies self-consciousness would detract from presence of the self in the world. In optimal presence, biologically and culturally determined cognitive processes are working in harmony to focus all levels of the self on events unfolding in the present situation in which the organism is situated, not on the *idea* of the self. We suggest that the same is also true for social presence. Maximum social presence produces *group flow*, typified by an immersion of self in the social world, and is a key to understanding the  creativity of groups in collaborative settings.

## The future of presence

We see presence evolving in two main directions. First, in virtual environments where the physical world is screened off from the individual, and a convincing synthetic experience is provided via immersive technology. Second, in computer-mediated interaction with the physical world, through virtual augmentation of, and tangible interaction with, real object and places. In both, there will be available a strong illusion of non-mediation.

In the former, the individual effectively experiences a perceptual illusion brought about by computer-generated images, sounds, and other sensations. In synthetic virtual reality, the immersive technology used will include a head-mounted display, which is becoming more affordable and beginning to reach a large market, replacing perception of the external physical world with that of a designed, interactive and computer-generated world. Multiple worlds are and will increasingly be available, supporting a wide range of experiences and activities: scientific visualization, psychotherapy, sports training, and entertainment, to name a few.

DOI: 10.1057/9781137431677.0009

In the latter, everyday perception of the physical world will be augmented with overlaid and intertwined computer-generated sights and sounds, but the individual experience will – at least in the short-term future – remain that of presence in the physical world. Blends of the proximal and the distal already occur in some situations, such as those provided by videoconferencing systems. As of now, these happen in specific physical places. But the trend towards mobile media access seems inevitable, and we can anticipate mediated meetings of physically distant and proximal people, each experiencing a consistent blended physical–virtual reality including all participants. For this to work, media devices will need to be sensitive to both the situational context of their use, and the state of their users. Presence levels will be adjusted dynamically during the management of blended streams of incoming and outgoing information.

Looking further ahead, we can expect almost all of our experiences to be mediated by information technology to some degree, in *human–computer confluence*. Any consideration of the future of human consciousness needs to take account of the coming importance of mediated presence. When integrated with the self, technology creates or modifies an external other of which it is not perceived to be a part. The external world itself will increasingly be an integrated blend of the physical and the virtual, the distal and the proximal. This brings the potential to choose between multiple perspectives on our own sense of self in relation to the world around us.

DOI: 10.1057/9781137431677.0009

# References

Alexander, R. D. (1990). Epigenetic rules and Darwinian algorithms. *Ethology and Sociobiology, 11*, 241–303.

Baars, B. J. (1988). *A Cognitive Theory of Consciousness*. New York: Cambridge University Press.

Bach-y-Rita, P., & Kercel, S. W. (2003). Sensory substitution and the human-machine interface. *Trends in Cognitive Neuroscience, 7*(12), 541–546.

Baddeley, A. (2012). Working memory: theories, models, and controversies. *Annual Review of Psychology, 63*, 1–29.

Bara, B. G., Ciaramidaro, A., Walter, H., & Adenzato, M. (2011). Intentional minds: a philosophical analysis of intention tested through FMRI experiments involving people with schizophrenia, people with autism, and healthy individuals. *Frontiers in Human Neuroscience, 5* 7.

Barsalou, L. W. (2002). Being there conceptually: simulating categories in preparation for situated action. In N. L. Stein, P. J. Bauer, & M. Rabinowitz (Eds.), *Representation, memory and development: essays in honor of Jean Mandler* (pp. 1–15). Mahwah, NJ: Erlbaum.

Barsalou, L. W. (2003). Situated simulation in the human conceptual system. *Language and Cognitive Processes, 18*, 513–562.

Becchio, C., & Bertone, C. (2005). Il paradosso dell'intenzionalità collettiva. *Giornale Italiano di Psicologia, 32*(4), 851–860.

Bechara, A., & Damasio, A. (2005). The somatic marker hypothesis: a neural theory of economic decision. *Games and Economic Behavior, 52*, 336–372.

DOI: 10.1057/9781137431677.0010

Benyon, D. (2012). Presence in blended spaces. *Interacting with Computers, 24*(4), 219–226.

Bereczkei, T. (2000). Evolutionary psychology: a new perspective in the behavioral sciences. *European Psychologist, 5*(3), 175–190.

Bernardet, U., Inderbitzin, M., Väljamäe, A., Mura, A., & Verschure, P. F. M. J. (2008). Validating presence by relying on recollection: human experience and performance in the mixed reality system XIM. In A. Spagnolli, & L. Gamberini (Eds.), *Proceedings of the 11th International Workshop on Presence* (pp. 178–182). Padova, Italy.

Bickhard, M. (2004). The dynamic emergence of representation. In H. Clapin, P. Staines & P. Slezak (Eds.), *Representation in mind: new approaches to mental representation* (pp. 71–90). Amsterdam: The Netherlands.

Biocca, F. (1997). The cyborg's dilemma: progressive embodiment in virtual environments. *Journal of Computer-Mediated Communications, 3*(2).

Biocca, F. A. (2003). Can we resolve the book, the physical reality, and the dream state problems? A three pole model of presence. Presentation at EU Presence Research Conference. Venice, Italy. May 7, 2003.

Biocca, F. A., & Rolland, J. P. (1998). Virtual eyes can rearrange your body: adaptation to visual displacement in see-through, head-mounted displays. *Presence, 7*, 262– 277.

Biocca, F. A., Harms, C., & Burgoon, J. K. (2003). Toward a more robust theory and measure of social presence: review and suggested criteria. *Presence: Teleoperators, and Virtual Environments, 12*(5), 456–480.

Blackmore, S. J. (1984). A psychological theory of the out-of-body experience. *Journal of Parapsychology, 48*, 201–218.

Blackmore, S. J. (1999). *The Meme Machine*. Oxford: Oxford University Press.

Blakemore, S. J., & Decety, J. (2001). From the perception of action to the understanding of intention. *Nature Reviews Neuroscience, 2*, 561–567.

Blakemore, S. J., Wolpert, D. M., & Frith, C. D. (2002). Abnormalities in the awareness of action. *Opinion in Trends in Cognitive Science, 6*(6), 237–242.

Blanke, O. (2012). Multisensory brain mechanisms of bodily self-consciousness. [Research Support, Non-U.S. Gov't].

DOI: 10.1057/9781137431677.0010

Botvinick, M., & Cohen, J. (1998). Rubber hands "feel" touch that the eye sees. *Nature, 391,* 756.

Bouchard, S., Dumoulin, S., Talbot, J. et al. (2012). Manipulating subjective realism and its impact on presence: preliminary results on feasibility and neuroanatomical correlates. *Interacting with Computers, 24*(4), 227–236.

Bracken, C., & Skalski, P. (2010) (Eds.) *Immersed in Media: Telepresence in Everyday Life.* New York: Routledge.

Bruner, J. (1991). *Acts of Meaning.* Jerusalem: Harvard University Press.

Bryant, D. J. (1997). Representing space in language and perception. *Mind & Language, 12*(3/4), 239–264.

Buss, D. M. (1995). Evolutionary psychology: a new paradigm for psychological science. *Psychological Inquiry, 6*(1), 1–30.

Castiello, U., Lusher, D., Burton, C. et al. (2004). Improving left hemispatial neglect using virtual reality. *Neurology, 62,* 1958–1962.

Chabris, C., & Simons, D. (2010). *The Invisible Gorilla: How Our Intuitions Deceive Us.* New York: Crown.

Ciaramidaro, A., Adenzato, M., Enrici, I., Erk, S., Pia, L., Bara, B. G. et al. (2007). The intentional network: how the brain reads varieties of intentions. *Neuropsychologia, 45*(13), 3105–3113.

Clark, A. (2003). *Natural Born Cyborgs: Minds, Technologies, and the Future of Human Intelligence.* Oxford: Oxford University Press.

Craig, A. D. (2002). How do you feel? Interoception: the sense of the physiological condition of the body. *Nature Reviews Neuroscience, 3*(8), 655–666.

Craig, A. D. (2003). Interoception: the sense of the physiological condition of the body. *Current Opinion in Neurobiology, 13*(4), 500–505.

Craig, A. D. (2010). The sentient self. *Brain Structure & Function, 214*(5–6), 563–577.

Crook, J. H. (1980). *The Evolution of Human Consciousness.* Oxford: Oxford University Press.

Crossley, M. L. (2000). *Introducing Narrative Psychology: Self, Trauma and the Construction of Meaning.* Buckingham: Open University Press.

Crossley, N. (2001). *The Social Body: Habit, Identity and Desire.* London: Sage.

Csikszentmihalyi, M. (1975). *Beyond Boredom and Anxiety.* San Francisco: Jossey-Bass.

Csikszentmihalyi, M. (1990). *Flow: The Psychology of Optimal Experience.* New York: HarperCollins.

DOI: 10.1057/9781137431677.0010

Csikszentmihalyi, M. (1994). *The Evolving Self.* New York: Harper Perennial.

Damasio, A. (1989). Time-locked multiregional retroactivation: a systems-level proposal for the neural substrates of recall and recognition. *Cognition, 33,* 25–62.

Damasio, A. (1994). *Decartes' Error: Emotion, Reason, and the Brain.* New York: Grosset/Putnam.

Damasio, A. (1999). *The Feeling of What Happens: Body, Emotion and the Making of Consciousness.* San Diego, CA: Harcourt Brace and Co, Inc.

Damasio, A. (2010). *Self Comes to Mind: Constructing the Conscious Brain.* New York: Pantheon Books.

Davies, C. (2003). Landscape, earth, body, being, space and time in the immersive virtual environments osmose and ephémère. In J. Malloy (Ed.), *Women in New Media.* Boston, USA: MIT Press.

Dawkins, R. (1989). *The Selfish Gene,* 2nd edn. Oxford: Oxford University Press.

Della Sala, S. (2005). The anarchic hand. *The Psychologist,* 18(10), 606–609.

Distin, K. (2005). *The Selfish Meme.* Cambridge: Cambridge University Press.

Dolan, R. J. (1999). Feeling the neurobiological self. *Nature, 401,* 847–848.

Dourish, P. (2001). *Where the Action Is: The Foundations of Embodied Interaction.* Cambridge, MA: MIT Press.

Durlik, C., Cardini, F., & Tsakiris, M. (2014). Being watched: the effect of social self-focus on interoceptive and exteroceptive somatosensory perception. *Consciousness and Cognition, 25,* 42–50.

Ehrsson, H. H. (2007). The experimental induction of out-of-body experiences. *Science, 317* (5841), 1048.

Epstein, S. (2008). Intuition from the perspective of cognitive-experiential self-theory. In H. Plessner, C. Betsch & T. Betsch (Eds.), *Intuition in Judgment and Decision Making* (pp. 23–37). New York: Lawrence Erlbaum Associates.

Eysenck, H. J. (1967). *The Biological Basis of Personality.* Springfield, IL: Charles C. Thomas.

Farnè, A., Bonifazi, S., & Làdavas, E. (2005). The role played by tool-use and tool-length on the plastic elongation of peri-hand space: a single case study. *Cognitive Neuropsychology,* 22(3–4), 408–418.

DOI: 10.1057/9781137431677.0010

Farné, A., Serino, A., & Làdavas, E. (2007). Dynamic size-change of perihand space following tool-use: determinants and spatial characteristics revealed through cross-modal extinction. *Cortex, 43*, 436–443.

Fauconnier, G., & Turner, M. (2002). *The Way We Think: Conceptual Blending and the Mind's Hidden Complexities.* New York: Basic Books.

Fletcher, P. C., & Frith, C. D. (2009). Perceiving is believing: a Bayesian approach to explaining the positive symptoms of schizophrenia. *Nature Reviews Neuroscience, 10*(1), pp. 48–58.

Freeman, D., Pugh, K., Antley, A., Slater, M., Bebbington, P., Gittins M., Dunn, G., Kuipers, E., Fowler, D., & Garety, P. (2008). Virtual reality study of paranoid thinking in the general population. *The British Journal of Psychiatry, 192*, pp. 258–263.

Frith, U., & de Vignemont, F. (2005). Egocentrism, allocentrism, and Asperger syndrome. *Consciousness and Cognition, 14*(4), 719–738.

Gaggioli, A., Mazzoni, E., Milani, L., & Riva, G. (in press). The creative link: investigating the relationship between social network indices, creative performance and flow in blended teams. *Computers in Human Behavior*, doi: 10.1016/j.chb.2013.1012.1003.

Gaggioli, A., Milani, L., Mazzoni, E., & Riva, G. (2011). Networked flow: a framework for understanding the dynamics of creative collaboration in educational and training settings. *The Open Education Journal, 4*(Suppl 2:M2), 107–115.

Gaggioli, A., Milani, L., Mazzoni, E., & Riva, G. (2013). *Networked Flow: Towards an Understanding of Creative Networks.* Dordrecht: Springer.

Galati, G., Lobel, E., Vallar, G., Berthoz, A., Pizzamiglio, L., & Le Bihan, D. (2000). The neural basis of egocentric and allocentric coding of space in humans: a functional magnetic resonance study. *Experimental Brain Research, 133*, 156–164.

Gallace, A., Ngo, M. K., Sulaitis, J., & Spence, C. (2011). Multisensory presence in virtual reality: possibilities & limitations. In G. Ghinea, F. Andres & S. R. Gulliver (Eds.), *Multiple Sensorial Media Advances and Applications: New Developments in MulSeMedia* (pp. 1–38). Hershey, PA: IGI Global.

Gallagher, R., & Jeannerod, M. (2002). From action to interaction. *Journal of Consciousness Studies, 9*, 3–26.

Gallagher, S. (2005). *How the Body Shapes the Mind.* New York: Oxford University Press.

DOI: 10.1057/9781137431677.0010

Gallese, V. (2003a). La molteplice natura delle relazioni interpersonali: la ricerca di un comune meccanismo neurofisiologico. *Networks, 1,* 24–47.

Gallese, V. (2003b). The roots of empathy: the shared mainfold hypothesis and the neural basis of intersubjectivity. *Psychopathology, 36,* 171–180.

Gallese, V. (2005). Embodied simulation: from neurons to phenomenal experience. *Phenomenology and the Cognitive Sciences, 4,* 23–48.

Gamberini, L., & Spagnolli, A. (2003). On the relationship between presence and usability: a situated, action-based approach to virtual environments. In G. Riva, W. A. IJsselsteijn & F. Davide (Eds.), *Being There: Concepts, Effects and Measurement of User Presence in Synthetic Environments* (pp. 97–107). Amsterdam: IOS Press. Online: http://www.emergingcommunication.com/volume105.html).

Garfinkel, S. N., & Critchley, H. D. (2013). Interoception, emotion and brain: new insights link internal physiology to social behaviour. Commentary on "Anterior insular cortex mediates bodily sensibility and social anxiety" by Terasawa et al. (2012). *Social Cognitive and Affective Neuroscience, 8*(3), 231–234.

Ghani, J. A., & Deshpande, S. P. (1994). Task characteristics and the experience of optimal flow in human-computer interaction. *The Journal of Psychology, 128*(4), 381–391.

Giudice, N. A., Klatzky, R. L., Bennett, C. R., & Loomis, J. M. (2013). Combining locations from working memory and long-term memory into a common spatial image. *Spatial Cognition & Computation: An Interdisciplinary Journal, 13*(2), 103–128.

Google Glass (2013). http://www.google.com/glass/start/. Accessed November 7, 2013.

Gregory, R. L. (1997). *Eye and Brain.* 5th edn. Oxford: Oxford University Press.

Haans, A., & IJsselsteijn, W. A. (2012). Embodiment and telepresence: toward a comprehensive theoretical framework. *Interacting with Computers, 24*(4), 211–218.

Haggard, P., & Clark, S. (2003). Intentional action: conscious experience and neural prediction. *Consciousness and Cognition, 12*(4), 695–707.

Haggard, P., Clark, S., & Kalogeras, J. (2002). Voluntary action and conscious awareness. *Nature Neuroscience, 5*(4), 382–385.

Heidegger, M. (1959). *Unterwegs zur Sprache.* Pfullingen: Neske.

DOI: 10.1057/9781137431677.0010

Hihara, S., Notoya, T., Tanaka, M., Ichinose, S., Ojima, H., Obayashi, S. et al. (2006). Extension of corticocortical afferents into the anterior bank of the intraparietal sulcus by tool-use training in adult monkeys. *Neuropsychologia, 44*(13), 2636–2646.

Hoffman, D. L., & Novak, T. P. (1996). Marketing in hypermedia computer mediated environments: conceptual foundations. *Journal of Marketing, 60*(July), 50–68.

Holmes N., & Spence, C. (2007). Dissociating body image and body schema with rubber hands. *Behavioral and Brain Sciences, 30*, 211–212.

Hommel, B., Müsseler, J., Aschersleben, G., & Prinz, W. (2001). The Theory of Event Coding (TEC): a framework for perception and action planning. *Behavioral and Brain Sciences, 24*(5), 849–937.

Hoshi, K., & Waterworth, J. A. (2009). Tangible presence in blended reality space, Presence 2009. Proceedings of the 12th Annual International Workshop on Presence. November 11–13, Los Angeles, CA, USA.

Hoshi, K., Öberg, F., & Nyberg, A. (2011) Designing blended reality space: conceptual foundations and applications. Proceedings of HCI 2011: The 25th BCS Conference on Human Computer Interaction. Newcastle Upon Tyne, UK, 4–8 July 2011, pp. 217–226.

Hutchins, E. (1996). *Cognition in the Wild*. Cambridge, MA: MIT Press.

Hutto, D. D. (2008). *Folk Psychological Narratives: The Sociocultural Basis of Understanding Reasons*. Cambridge, MA: MIT Press.

Ihde, D. (1990). *Technology and the Lifeworld – From Garden to Earth*. Bloomington and Indianapolis: Indiana University Press.

IJsselsteijn, W. A., de Kort, Y. A. W., & Haans, A. (2006). Is this my hand I see before me? The rubber hand illusion in reality, virtual reality, and mixed reality. *Presence: Teleoperators and Virtual Environments, 15*, 455–464.

Imaz, M., & Benyon, D. (2006). *Designing with Blends: Conceptual Foundations of Human-Computer Interaction and Software Engineering*. Cambridge, MA: MIT Press.

Iriki, A., Tanaka, M., & Iwamura, Y. (1996). Coding of modified body schema during tool use by macaque postcentral neurones. *Neuroreport, 7*(14), 2325–2330.

Iriki, A., Tanaka, M., Obayashi, S., & Iwamura, Y. (2001). Self-images in the video monitor coded by monkey intraparietal neurons. *Neuroscience Research, 40*(2), 163–173.

James, W. (1890). *The Principles of Psychology*. New York: Holt.

DOI: 10.1057/9781137431677.0010

Jäncke, L., Cheetham, M., & Baumgartner, T. (2009). *Virtual reality and the role of the prefrontal cortex in adults and children. Frontiers in Neuroscience, 3*(1), 52–59.

Janoff-Bulman, R., & Frantz, C. M. (1997). The impact of trauma on meaning: from meaningless world to meaningful life. In M. Power & C. R. Brewin (Eds.), *The transformation of meaning in psychological therapies* (pp. 91–106). New York: Wiley.

Kahneman, D. (2002). Maps of bounded rationality: a perspective on intuitive judgment and choice. In T. Frängsmyr (Ed.), *The Nobel Prizes 2002* (pp. 449–489). Stockholm: Nobel Foundation.

Kaptelinin, V. (1996). Computer-mediated activity: functional organs in social and developmental contexts. In B. Nardi (Ed.), *Context and consciousness: Activity theory and human-computer interaction* (pp. 45–68). Cambridge, MA: MIT Press.

Kaptelinin, V., & Nardi, B. (2006). *Acting with Technology: Activity Theory and Interaction Design.* Cambridge, MA: MIT Press.

Kåver, A., & Nilsonne, Å. (2002) *Dialektisk beteendeterapi vid emotionellt instabil personlighetsstörining – Teori, strategi och teknik.* Natur och Kultur, Sweden (in Swedish only).

Kelly, J. W., & Avraamides, M. N. (2011). Cross-sensory transfer of reference frames in spatial memory. *Cognition, 118*(3), 444–450.

Kihlstrom, J. F. (1987). The cognitive unconscious. *Science, 237*(4821), 1445–1452.

Kjellgren, A., Sundequist, U., Sundholm, U., Norlander, T., & Archer, T. (2004). Altered consciousness in flotation-REST and chamber-REST: experience of experimental pain and subjective stress. *Social Behaviour and Personality, 32*, 103–115.

Knill, D. C., & Pouget, A. (2004). The Bayesian brain: the role of uncertainty in neural coding and computation. *Trends in Neurosciences, 27*(12), 712–719.

Knoblich, G., & Flach, R. (2003). Action identity: evidence from self-recognition, prediction, and coordination. *Consciousness and Cognition, 12*, 620–632.

Knoblich, G., Thornton, I., Grosjean, M., & Shiffrar, M. (Eds.). (2005). *Human Body Perception from the Inside Out.* New York: Oxford University Press.

Koriat, A. (2007). Metacognition and consciousness. In P. D. Zelaso, M. Moscovitch & E. Thompson (Eds.), *Cambridge Handbook of Consciousness* (pp. 289–325). New York: Cambridge University Press.

DOI: 10.1057/9781137431677.0010

Koriat, A., & Levy-Sadot, R. (1999). Processes underlying metacognitive judgments: information-based and experience-based monitoring of one's own knowledge. In C. Shelly & T. Yaacov (Eds.), *Dual-process theories in social psychology* (pp. 483–502). New York: Guilford Press.

Laarni, J., Ravaja, N., Saari, T., & Hartmann, T. (2004). Personality-related differences in subjective presence. Proceedings of Presence 2004. Valencia, Spain, October 2004.

Lakoff, G., & Johnson, M. (1980). *Metaphors We Live By.* Chicago: The University of Chicago Press.

Lenggenhager, B., Tadi, T., Metzinger, T. et al. (2007). Video ergo sum: manipulating bodily self-consciousness. *Science, 317*(5841), 1096–1099.

Leontjev, A. N. (1978). *Activity, Consciousness, and Personality.* Englewood, NJ: Prentice-Hall. Online: http://marxists.org/archive/leontev/works/1978/ch3.htm.

Leontjev, A. N. (1981). *Problems of the Development of Mind.* Moscow: Progress.

Lindner, M., Hundhammer, T., Ciaramidaro, A., Linden, D. E., & Mussweiler, T. (2008). The neural substrates of person comparison – an fMRI study. *Neuroimage, 40*(2), 963–971.

Llinás, R. R. (2001). *I of the Vortex: From Neurons to Self.* Cambridge, MA: MIT Press.

Lombard, M., & Ditton, T. (1997). At the heart of it all: the concept of presence. *Journal of Computer Mediated Communication, 3*(2). Online: http://jcmc.indiana.edu/vol3/issue2/lombard.html. Accessed September, 2009.

Longo, M. R., & Haggard, P. (2010). An implicit body representation underlying human position sense. *Proceedings of the National Academy of Sciences, 107*(26), 11727–11732.

Longo, M. R., Azañón, L., & Haggard, P. (2010). More than skin deep: body representation beyond primary somatosensory cortex. *Neuropsychologia, 48*, 655–668.

Loomis, J. M., Klatzky, R. L., & Giudice, N. A. (2013). Representing 3D space in working memory: spatial images from vision, hearing, touch, and language. In S. Lacey & R. Lawson (Eds.), *Multisensory Imagery* (pp. 131–155). New York: Springer.

Loomis, J. M., Klatzky, R. L., Avraamides, M. N., Lippa, Y., & Golledge, R. G. (2007). Functional equivalence of spatial images produced by perception and spatial language. In F. Mast & L. Jancke (Eds.), *Spatial*

DOI: 10.1057/9781137431677.0010

*processing in navigation, imagery, and perception* (pp. 29–48). New York: Springer.

Loomis, J. M., Lippa, Y., Golledge, R. G., & Klatzky, R. L. (2002). Spatial updating of locations specified by 3-D sound and spatial language. *Journal of Experimental Psychology: Learning, Memory, and Cognition, 28*(2), 335–345.

Maravita, A., & Iriki, A. (2004). Tools for the body (schema). *Trends in Cognitive Sciences, 8*(2), 79–86.

Marsh, T. (2003). Staying there: an activity-based approach to narrative design and evaluation as an antidote to virtual corpsing. In G. Riva, F. Davide & W. A. IJsselsteijn (Eds.), *Being there: concepts, effects and measurements of user presence in synthetic environments* (pp. 85–96). Amsterdam: IOS Press.

Massimini, F., & Delle Fave, A. (2000). Individual development in a bio-cultural perspective. *American Psychologist, 55*(1), 24–33.

Matelli, M., & Luppino, G. (2001). Parietofrontal circuits for action and space perception in the macaque monkey. *Neuroimage, 14*(1 Pt 2), S27–S32.

Meltzoff, A. N., & Decety, J. (2003). What imitation tells us about social cognition: a rapprochement between developmental psychology and cognitive neuroscience. *Philosophical Transactions of the Royal Society, 358*, 491–500.

Meltzoff, A. N., & Moore, M. K. (1977). Imitation of facial and manual gestures by human neonates. *Science, 198*, 702–709.

Merleau-Ponty, M. (1962). *The Phenomenology of Perception.* Translated by Colin Smith. London: Routledge and Keegan Paul.

Merriam-Webster (2010). *The Merriam-Webster Dictionary.* Springfield, MA: Merriam-Webster.

Metzinger, T. (1999). The hint half guessed. *Scientific American, 11*, 184–189.

Metzinger, T. (2006). Reply to Gallagher: different conceptions of embodiment, *Psyche* 12(4).

Minsky, M. (1980). Telepresence. *Omni Magazine*, June 1980.

Misselhorn, C. (2009). Empathy with inanimate objects and the uncanny valley. *Minds and Machines, 19*(3), 345–359.

Moller, H., & Barbera, J. (2006). Media presence, consciousness and dreaming. In G. Riva, M. T. Anguera, B. K. Wiederhold, and F. Mantovani (Eds.), *From communication to presence: cognition, emotions*

DOI: 10.1057/9781137431677.0010

*and culture towards the ultimate communicative experience* (Festschrift in honor of Luigi Anolli). Amsterdam: IOS Press.

Morganti, F., & Riva, G. (2004). Ambient intelligence in rehabilitation. In G. Riva, F. Davide, F. Vatalaro & M. Alcañiz (Eds.), *Ambient intelligence: the evolution of technology, communication and cognition towards the future of the human-computer interaction* (pp. 283–295). Amsterdam: IOS Press. Online: http://www.emergingcommunication. com/volume6.html.

Nagel, T. (1974). What is it like to be a bat? *Philosophical Review*, *83*(4), 435–450.

Nardi, B. (Ed.). (1996). *Context and Consciousness: Activity Theory and Human-Computer Interaction*. Cambridge, MA: MIT Press.

Nath, S. (2001). Emotion based narratives: a new approach to creating story experiences in immersive virtual environments. MA Thesis, Central Saint Martin's College of Art and Design, London, UK.

Newcombe, N. S., & Huttenlocher, J. (2000). *Making Space: The Development of Spatial Representation and Reasoning*. Cambridge, MA: MIT Press.

New Scientist (2010). The Real Avatar: Body Transfer Turns Men into Girls. May 13. http://www.newscientist.com/article/dn18896-the-real-avatar-body-transfer-turns-men-into-girls.html. Accessed June 27, 2013.

Norman, D. A. (1993). *Things that Make Us Smart*. Reading, Mass: Addison-Wesley.

Normand, J.-M., Giannopoulos, E. Spanlang, E. B. et al. (2011). Multisensory stimulation can induce an illusion of larger belly size in immersive virtual reality. *PLoS One*, *6*(1): e16128.

Ohayon, M. M., Zulley, J., Guilleminault, C., & Smirne, S. (1999) Prevalence and pathologic associations of sleep paralysis in the general population. *Neurology*, *52*: 1194.

Pacherie, E. (2006). Toward a dynamic theory of intentions. In S. Pockett, W. P. Banks & S. Gallagher (Eds.), *Does consciousness cause behavior?* (pp. 145–167). Cambridge, MA: MIT Press.

Pacherie, E. (2008). The phenomenology of action: a conceptual framework. *Cognition*, *107*(1), 179–217.

Petkova, V. I., & Ehrsson, H. H. (2008). If I were you: perceptual illusion of body swapping. *PLoS One*, *3*(12): e3832.

DOI: 10.1057/9781137431677.0010

Petranker, J. (2003). Inhabiting conscious experience: engaged objectivity in the first-person study of consciousness. *Journal of Consciousness Studies, 10*(12), 3–23.

Pfeiffer, C., Lopez, C., Schmutz, V., Duenas, J. A., Martuzzi, R., & Blanke, O. (2013). Multisensory origin of the subjective first-person perspective: visual, tactile, and vestibular mechanisms. *PLoS One, 8*(4), e61751.

Previc, F. H. (1998). The neuropsychology of 3-D space. *Psychological Bulletin, 124*(2), 123–164.

Price, M. C., & Norman, E. (2008). Intuitive decisions on the fringes of consciousness: are they conscious and does it matter? *Judgment and Decision Making, 3*(1), 28–41.

Prinz, J. (2006). Putting the brakes on enactive perception. *Psyche, 12*(1), 1–12. Online: http://psyche.cs.monash.edu.au.

Prinz, W. (1997). Perception and action planning. *European Journal of Cognitive Psychology, 9*(2), 129–154.

Reber, A. S. (1989). Implicit learning and tacit knowledge. *Journal of Experimental Psychology: General, 118*(3), 219–235.

Riva, G. (1998). Modifications of body-image induced by virtual reality. *Perceptual & Motor Skills, 86*(1), 163–170.

Riva, G. (2004). The psychology of ambient intelligence: activity, situation and presence. In G. Riva, F. Davide, F. Vatalaro & M. Alcañiz (Eds.), *Ambient intelligence: the evolution of technology, communication and cognition towards the future of the human-computer interaction* (pp. 19–34). Amsterdam: IOS Press. Online: http://www.emergingcommunication.com/volume6.html.

Riva, G. (2006). Being-in-the-world-with: presence meets social and cognitive neuroscience. In G. Riva, M. T. Anguera, B. K. Wiederhold & F. Mantovani (Eds.), *From communication to presence: cognition, emotions and culture towards the ultimate communicative experience. Festschrift in honor of Luigi Anolli* (pp. 47–80). Amsterdam: IOS Press. Online: http://www.emergingcommunication.com/volume8.html.

Riva, G. (2008). Enacting interactivity: the role of presence. In F. Morganti, A. Carassa & G. Riva (Eds.), *Enacting intersubjectivity: a cognitive and social perspective on the study of interactions* (pp. 97–114). Amsterdam: IOS Press: Online: http://www.emergingcommunication.com/volume10.html.

Riva, G. (2009). Is presence a technology issue? Some insights from cognitive sciences *Virtual Reality, 13*(3), 59–69.

DOI: 10.1057/9781137431677.0010

Riva, G., & Mantovani, F. (2012a). Being there: understanding the feeling of presence in a synthetic environment and its potential for clinical change. In C. Eichenberg (Ed.), *Virtual reality in psychological, medical and pedagogical applications*, (pp. 3–34). New York: InTech. Online: http://www.intechopen.com/books/virtual-reality-in-psychological-medical-and-pedagogical-applications/being-there-understanding-the-feeling-of-presence-in-a-synthetic-environment-and-its-potential-for-c).

Riva, G., & Mantovani, F. (2012b). From the body to the tools and back: a general framework for presence in mediated interactions. *Interacting with Computers*, 24(4), 203–210.

Riva, G., & Mantovani, F. (2014). Extending the self through the tools and the others: a general framework for presence and social presence in mediated interactions. In G. Riva, J. A. Waterworth & D. Murray (Eds.), *Interacting with presence: HCI and the sense of presence in computer-mediated environments* (pp. 12–34). Berlin: De Gruyter Open. Online: http://www.presence-research.com.

Riva, G., & Waterworth, J. A. (2003). Presence and the self: a cognitive neuroscience approach. *Presence-Connect*, 3(1), Online: http://presence.cs.ucl.ac.uk/presenceconnect/articles/Apr2003/jwworthApr72003114532/jwworthApr72003114532.html.

Riva, G., Davide, F., & IJsselsteijn, W. A. (Eds.) (2003). *Being There: Concepts, Effects and Measurements of User Presence in Synthetic Environments*. Amsterdam: IOS Press. Online: http://www.emergingcommunication.com/volume5.html.

Riva, G., Waterworth, J. A., & Waterworth, E. L. (2004). The layers of presence: a bio-cultural approach to understanding presence in natural and mediated environments. *Cyberpsychology & Behavior*, 7(4), 405–419.

Riva, G., Waterworth, J. A., Waterworth, E. L., & Mantovani, F. (2011). From intention to action: the role of presence. *New Ideas in Psychology*, 29(1), 24–37.

Rizzolatti, G., & Sinigaglia, C. (2006). *So quel che fai. Il cervello che agisce e i neuroni specchio*. Milano: Raffaello Cortina.

Rizzolatti, G., Fadiga, L., Gallese, V., & Fogassi, L. (1996). Premotor cortex and the recognition of motor actions. *Cognitive Brain Research*, 3, 131–141.

Rollo, D. (2007). *Narrazione e sviluppo psicologico. Aspetti cognitivi, affettivi e sociali*. Roma: Carocci.

DOI: 10.1057/9781137431677.0010

Russell, J. A. (1996). *Agency: Its Role in Mental Development*. Hove: Erlbaum.

Safran, J. D., & Greenberg, L. S. (1991). *Emotion, Psychotherapy, and Change*. New York: The Guilford Press.

Searle, J. (1983). *Intentionality: An Essay in the Philosophy of Mind*. New York: Cambridge University Press.

Searle, J. (1990). Collective intentions and actions. In P. Cohen, J. Morgan & M. E. Pollack (Eds.), *Intentions in Communication* (pp. 401–416). Cambridge, MA: Bradford Books.

Searle, J. (2004). *Mind: A Brief Introduction*. Oxford: Oxford University Press.

Selman, B., & Kautz, H. (1996). Knowledge compilation and theory approximation. *Journal of the ACM, 43*(2), 193–224.

Shilling, C. (2012). *The Body & Social Theory*. London: Sage.

Simmons, K. W., & Barsalou, L. W. (2003). The similarity-in-topography principle: reconciling theories of conceptual deficits. *Cognitive Neuropsychology, 20*, 451–486.

Slater, M. & Steed, A. J. (2000). A virtual presence counter. *Presence: Teleoperators and Virtual Environments, 9*(5), 413–434.

Slater, M., Lotto, B., Arnold, M. M., & Sanchez-Vives, M. V. (2009). How we experience immersive virtual environments: the concept of presence and its measurement. *Anuario de Psicología, 40*(2), 193–210.

Slater, M., Perez-Marcos, D. Ehrsson, H. H. et al. (2008). Towards a digital body: the virtual arm illusion. *Frontiers in Human Neuroscience, 2*(6), 1–8.

Slater, M., Spanlang, B. Sanchez-Vives, M. V. et al. (2010). First person experience of body transfer in virtual reality. *PLoS One, 5*(5): e10564.

Slaughter, V., & Brownell, C. (Eds.). (2012). *Early Development of Body Representations*. Cambridge, UK: Cambridge University Press.

Spagnolli, A., & Gamberini, L. (2002, 9–11 October). Immersion/emersion: presence in hybrid environments. Paper presented at the Presence 2002: Fifth Annual International Workshop, Porto, Portugal.

Stanovich, K. E., & West, R. F. (2000). Individual differences in reasoning: implications for the rationality debate? *Behavioral and Brain Sciences, 23*(5), 645–665.

The vOICe (2014). http://www.seeingwithsound.com. Accessed January 30, 2014.

DOI: 10.1057/9781137431677.0010

Trevino, L. K., & Webster, J. (1992). Flow in computer-mediated communication. *Communication Research, 19*(5), 539–573.

Tsakiris, M., Longo, M. R., & Haggard, P. (2010). Having a body versus moving your body: neural signatures of agency and body-ownership. [Research Support, Non-U.S. Gov't]. *Neuropsychologia, 48*(9), 2740–2749.

Turner, V. (1982). *From Ritual to Theater: The Human Seriousness of Play.* New York: PAJ Publications.

van Beers, R. J., Sittig, A. C., & van der Gon, J. J. (1996). How humans combine simultaneous proprioceptive and visual position information. *Experimental Brain Research, 111*(2), 253–261.

van Beers, R. J., Sittig, A. C., & van der Gon, J. J. (1999). Integration of proprioceptive and visual position-information: an experimentally supported model. *Journal of Neurophysiology, 81*(3), 1355–1364.

van Beers, R. J., Wolpert, D. M., & Haggard, P. (2002). When feeling is more important than seeing in sensorimotor adaptation. *Current Biology, 12*(10), 834–837.

Vilares, I., & Kording, K. (2011). Bayesian models: the structure of the world, uncertainty, behavior, and the brain. [Research Support, N.I.H., Extramural].

Villani, D., Riva, F., Waterworth, E. L., Waterworth, J., Freeman, J., & Riva, G. (2005). Virtual Reality to Reduce Anxiety in Healthy Populations: The Relaxation Island CyberTherapy, Basel, Switzerland, June 2005.

Vogeley, K., & Fink, G. R. (2003). Neural correlates of the first-person-perspective. *Trends in Cognitive Sciences, 7*(1), 38–42.

Walter, H., Abler, B., Ciaramidaro, A., & Erk, S. (2005). Motivating forces of human actions: neuroimaging reward and social interaction. *Brain Research Bulletin, 67*(5), 368–381.

Walter, H., Adenzato, M., Ciaramidaro, A., Enrici, I., Pia, L., & Bara, B. G. (2004). Understanding intentions in social interaction: the role of the anterior paracingulate cortex. *Journal of Cognitive Neuroscience, 16*(10), 1854–1863.

Walter, H., Ciaramidaro, A., Adenzato, M., Vasic, N., Ardito, R. B., Erk, S. et al. (2009). Dysfunction of the social brain in schizophrenia is modulated by intention type: an fMRI study. *Social Cognitive and Affective Neuroscience, 4*(2), 166–176.

Waskan, J. (2006). *Models and Cognition.* Cambridge, MA: MIT Press.

DOI: 10.1057/9781137431677.0010

Waterworth, E. L. & Waterworth, J. A. (2001). Focus, locus and sensus: the 3 dimensions of virtual experience. *Cyberpsychology and Behavior*, 4(2), 203–214.

Waterworth, E. L., Häggkvist, M., Jalkanen, K., Olsson, S., Waterworth, J. A., & Wimelius, H. (2003). The exploratorium: an environment to explore your feelings. *PsychNology Journal*, 1(3), 189–201.

Waterworth, E. L., Waterworth, J. A., Häggqvist, M., Jalkanen, K., Olsson, S., Wimelius, H., & Yttergren, B. (2004). Mood devices: interactive media and mental health. Proceedings of e-Society 2004, Avila, Spain, July 2004.

Waterworth, J. A. (1997). Creativity and sensation: the case for synaesthetic media. *Leonardo*, 30(4), 327–330.

Waterworth, J. A. (2003). Virtual realisation: supporting creative outcomes in medicine and music. *PsychNology Journal*, 1(4), 410–427.

Waterworth, J. A., & Fällman, D. (2003). The reality helmet: transforming the experience of being-in-the-world. Proceedings of HCI 2003: Designing for Society, Bath, UK, Volume 2, 191–194.

Waterworth, J. A., & Waterworth, E. L. (2003). The core of presence: presence as perceptual illusion. *Presence-Connect*, 3(3).

Waterworth, J. A., & Waterworth, E. L. (2004). Relaxation island: A virtual tropical paradise. Interactive experience. Proceedings of BCS HCI2004: Designing for Life, Leeds, UK, September 2004.

Waterworth, J. A. & Waterworth, E. L. (2014). Altered, expanded and distributed embodiment: three categories of Interactive presence. In G. Riva, J. A. Waterworth & D. Murray (Eds.), *Interacting with presence: HCI and the sense of presence in computer-mediated environments* (pp. 12–34). Berlin: De Gruyter Open.

Waterworth, J. A., Waterworth E. L., Mantovani, F. et al. (2010). On feeling (the) present: an evolutionary account of the sense of presence in physical and electronically-mediated environments. *Journal of Consciousness Studies*, 17(1–2), 167–189.

Waterworth, J. A., Waterworth, E. L., & Westling, J. (2002, 9–11 October). Presence as Performance: the mystique of digital participation. Paper presented at the Presence 2002: Fifth Annual International Workshop, Porto, Portugal.

Wilson, M. (2006). Covert imitation. In G. Knoblich, I. M. Thornton, M. Grosjean & M. Shiffrar (Eds.), *Human body perception from the inside out* (pp. 211–228). New York: Oxford University Press.

DOI: 10.1057/9781137431677.0010

Wilson, M., & Knoblich, G. (2005). The case for motor involvement in perceiving conspecifics. *Psychological Bulletin, 131*(3), 460–473.

Winograd, T., & Flores, F. (1986). *Understanding Computers and Cognition: A New Foundation for Design.* Norwood, NJ: Ablex Publishing Corporation.

Wirth, W., Hartmann, T., Bocking, S., Vorderer, P., Klimmt, C., Schramm, H. et al. (2007). A process model of the formation of spatial presence experiences. *Media Psychology, 9*(3), 493–525.

Wolbers, T., Klatzky, R. L., Loomis, J. M., Wutte, M. G., & Giudice, N. A. (2011). Modality-independent coding of spatial layout in the human brain. *Current Biology, 21*(11), 984–989.

Yee, N., & Bailenson, J. N. (2007). The Proteus effect: self transformations in virtual reality. *Human Communication Research, 33,* 271–290.

Zahoric, P., & Jenison, R. L. (1998). Presence as being-in-the-world. *Presence, Teleoperators, and Virtual Environments, 7*(1), 78–89.

DOI: 10.1057/9781137431677.0010

# Index

absence, 26, 70
absorption states, 29
action, 36, 52
activity, 36
*Activity Theory*, 38
allocentric approach, 31
allocentric frame, 60
*altered embodiment*, 66
anticipation, 37
anxiety. *See* psychological
 problems
as if body-loop, 32
attention, 26–28
 focus of, 26
 focused, 69

bat
 what it feels like to be one,
 83
being there, 11
bimodal neurons, 47
*blended reality*, 13
*blended reality space*, 72
*blending theory*, 72
blends, 73
blind man's stick, 80
bodily self-consciousness, vi,
 54, 55, 105
body image, 80
body schema, 80
breakdowns, 28, 29, 30, 31,
 51, 63
breakdowns in presence, 28–31,
 67

*canonical* neurons, 47
CEST. *See* cognitive-
 experiential self-theory
cognitive evolution, 19, 43, 44
cognitive load, 76
collective intentions, 40
Common Coding Theory, 47,
 56
communicative context, 76–78
*Convergence Zone Theory*, 57
*Covert Imitation Theory*, 48, 51
cyber-sickness, 26
cyborgs, 14

depersonalization/
 derealization, 30
depression. *See* psychological
 problems
desktop metaphor, 74
*digital participation*, 71
D-intentions. *See* distal
 intentions
distal intentions, 39, 42
distributed cognition, 14
*distributed embodiment*, 67, 81
dreaming, 28

egocentric approach, 31
*egocentric frame*, 59
*embodied immersion*, 71
embodiment, 64–89
 *altered*, 72–76
 *distributed*, 81–83
 *expanded*, 67–68

DOI: 10.1057/9781137431677.0011

DOI: 10.1057/9781137431677.0011